Learning React Native

Building Mobile Applications with JavaScript

Bonnie Eisenman

Beijing · Boston · Farnham · Sebastopol · Tokyo

Learning React Native

by Bonnie Eisenman

Printed in the United States of America.

Published by O'Reilly Media, Inc., 1005 Gravenstein Highway North, Sebastopol, CA 95472.

O'Reilly books may be purchased for educational, business, or sales promotional use. Online editions are also available for most titles (*http://safaribooksonline.com*). For more information, contact our corporate/institutional sales department: 800-998-9938 or *corporate@oreilly.com*.

Editor: Meg Foley
Production Editor: Nicholas Adams
Copyeditor: Jasmine Kwityn
Proofreader: Christina Edwards

Indexer: Ellen Troutman-Zaig
Interior Designer: David Futato
Cover Designer: Randy Comer
Illustrator: Rebecca Demarest

December 2015:   First Edition

Revision History for the First Edition
2015-12-01:   First Release

See *http://oreilly.com/catalog/errata.csp?isbn=9781491929001* for release details.

978-1-491-92900-1

[LSI]

This book assumes you are developing on OS X. Developing on OS X is a requirement for writing iOS apps. Linux and Windows support for writing Android applications is a work-in-progress. You can read more about Linux and Android support here (*https://facebook.github.io/react-native/docs/linux-windows-support.html*).

Conventions Used in This Book

The following typographical conventions are used in this book:

Italic
: Indicates new terms, URLs, email addresses, filenames, and file extensions.

`Constant width`
: Used for program listings, as well as within paragraphs to refer to program elements such as variable or function names, databases, data types, environment variables, statements, and keywords.

`Constant width bold`
: Shows commands or other text that should be typed literally by the user.

`Constant width italic`
: Shows text that should be replaced with user-supplied values or by values determined by context.

This element signifies a tip or suggestion.

This element signifies a general note.

This element indicates a warning or caution.

Preface

This book is an introduction to React Native, Facebook's JavaScript framework for building mobile applications. Using your existing knowledge of JavaScript and React, you'll be able to build and deploy fully featured mobile applications for both iOS and Android that truly render natively. Just because it's JavaScript doesn't mean we should settle for less. There are plenty of advantages to working with React Native over traditional means of mobile development, and we don't need to sacrifice the native look and feel.

We'll start with the basics, and work our way up to deploying a full-fledged application to both the iOS App Store and the Google Play Store, with 100% code reuse between the two platforms. In addition to the essentials of the framework, we'll discuss how to work beyond it, including how to make use of third-party libraries and even how to write your own Java or Objective-C libraries to extend React Native.

If you're coming to mobile development from the perspective of a frontend software engineer or web developer, this is the book for you. React Native is a pretty amazing thing, and I hope you're as excited to explore it as I am!

Prerequisites

This book is not an introduction to React, in general. We'll assume that you have some working knowledge of React. If you're brand new to React, I suggest reading through a tutorial or two before coming back to take the plunge into mobile development. Specifically, you should be familiar with the role of props and state, the component lifecycle, and how to create React components.

We'll also be using some ES6 syntax, as well as JSX. If you aren't familiar with these, don't worry; we'll cover JSX in Chapter 2, and ES6 syntax in Appendix A. These features are essentially 1:1 translations of the JavaScript code you're already accustomed to writing.

Table of Contents

Using Code Examples

Supplemental material (code examples, exercises, etc.) is available for download at: *https://github.com/bonniee/learning-react-native*.

This book is here to help you get your job done. In general, if example code is offered with this book, you may use it in your programs and documentation. You do not need to contact us for permission unless you're reproducing a significant portion of the code. For example, writing a program that uses several chunks of code from this book does not require permission. Selling or distributing a CD-ROM of examples from O'Reilly books does require permission. Answering a question by citing this book and quoting example code does not require permission. Incorporating a significant amount of example code from this book into your product's documentation does require permission.

We appreciate, but do not require, attribution. An attribution usually includes the title, author, publisher, and ISBN. For example: "*Learning React Native* by Bonnie Eisenman (O'Reilly). Copyright 2016 Bonnie Eisenman, 978-1-491-92900-1."

If you feel your use of code examples falls outside fair use or the permission given above, feel free to contact us at *permissions@oreilly.com*.

Safari® Books Online

Safari Books Online is an on-demand digital library that delivers expert content in both book and video form from the world's leading authors in technology and business.

Technology professionals, software developers, web designers, and business and creative professionals use Safari Books Online as their primary resource for research, problem solving, learning, and certification training.

Safari Books Online offers a range of plans and pricing for enterprise, government, education, and individuals.

Members have access to thousands of books, training videos, and prepublication manuscripts in one fully searchable database from publishers like O'Reilly Media, Prentice Hall Professional, Addison-Wesley Professional, Microsoft Press, Sams, Que, Peachpit Press, Focal Press, Cisco Press, John Wiley & Sons, Syngress, Morgan Kaufmann, IBM Redbooks, Packt, Adobe Press, FT Press, Apress, Manning, New Riders, McGraw-Hill, Jones & Bartlett, Course Technology, and hundreds more. For more information about Safari Books Online, please visit us online.

How to Contact Us

Please address comments and questions concerning this book to the publisher:

O'Reilly Media, Inc.
1005 Gravenstein Highway North
Sebastopol, CA 95472
800-998-9938 (in the United States or Canada)
707-829-0515 (international or local)
707-829-0104 (fax)

We have a web page for this book, where we list errata, examples, and any additional information. You can access this page at *http://bit.ly/learning-react-native*.

To comment or ask technical questions about this book, send email to *bookquestions@oreilly.com*.

For more information about our books, courses, conferences, and news, see our website at *http://www.oreilly.com*.

Find us on Facebook: *http://facebook.com/oreilly*

Follow us on Twitter: *http://twitter.com/oreillymedia*

Watch us on YouTube: *http://www.youtube.com/oreillymedia*

Resources

It's dangerous to go alone! Well, not really, but that doesn't mean you have to. Here are some resources you may find useful as you work through the book:

- The GitHub repository (*https://github.com/bonniee/learning-react-native*) for this book contains all of the code samples we'll be discussing. If you get stumped, or want more context, try looking here first.

- Join the mailing list at LearningReactNative.com (*http://learningreactnative.com*) for follow-up articles, suggestions, and helpful resources.

- The official documentation (*https://facebook.github.io/react-native/*) has a lot of good reference material.

Additionally, the React Native community is a useful resource:

- Brent Vatne's React Native newsletter (*http://bit.ly/react-native-newsletter*)
- The react-native tag on Stack Overflow (*http://bit.ly/react-native-so*)
- #reactnative (*irc://chat.freenode.net/reactnative*) on Freenode

Acknowledgments

As is traditional: this book would not have been possible without the help and support of many others. Thank you to my editor, Meg Foley, and the rest of the O'Reilly team, for bringing this project into the world. Thank you also to my technical reviewers, for your time and insightful feedback: David Bieber, Jason Brown, Erica Portnoy, and Jonathan Stark. I would also like to thank the React Native team, without whose stellar work this book would naturally be impossible. Thanks also to Zachary Elliot for his help with the Zebreto application and Android in general.

And many thanks are owed to my dear friends, who put up with me throughout this process and provided moral support, guidance, and distraction, as the situation required. Thank you.

CHAPTER 1

What Is React Native?

React Native is a JavaScript framework for writing real, natively rendering mobile applications for iOS and Android. It's based on React, Facebook's JavaScript library for building user interfaces, but instead of targeting the browser, it targets mobile platforms. In other words: web developers can now write mobile applications that look and feel truly "native," all from the comfort of a JavaScript library that we already know and love. Plus, because most of the code you write can be shared between platforms, React Native makes it easy to simultaneously develop for both Android and iOS.

Similar to React for the Web, React Native applications are written using a mixture of JavaScript and XML-esque markup, known as JSX. Then, under the hood, the React Native "bridge" invokes the native rendering APIs in Objective-C (for iOS) or Java (for Android). Thus, your application will render using real mobile UI components, *not* webviews, and will look and feel like any other mobile application. React Native also exposes JavaScript interfaces for platform APIs, so your React Native apps can access platform features like the phone camera, or the user's location.

React Native currently supports both iOS and Android, and has the potential to expand to future platforms as well. In this book, we'll cover both iOS and Android. The vast majority of the code we write will be cross-platform. And yes: you can really use React Native to build production-ready mobile applications! Some anecdota: Facebook (*http://bit.ly/1YipO7A*), Palantir (*http://bit.ly/1PPEiZH*), and TaskRabbit (*http://bit.ly/1PPEjNg*) are already using it in production for user-facing applications.

Advantages of React Native

The fact that React Native actually renders using its host platform's standard rendering APIs enables it to stand out from most existing methods of cross-platform application development, like Cordova or Ionic. Existing methods of writing mobile applications using combinations of JavaScript, HTML, and CSS typically render using webviews. While this approach can work, it also comes with drawbacks, especially around performance. Additionally, they do not usually have access to the host platform's set of native UI elements. When these frameworks do try to mimic native UI elements, the results usually "feel" just a little off; reverse-engineering all the fine details of things like animations takes an enormous amount of effort, and they can quickly become out of date.

In contrast, React Native actually translates your markup to real, native UI elements, leveraging existing means of rendering views on whatever platform you are working with. Additionally, React works separately from the main UI thread, so your application can maintain high performance without sacrificing capability. The update cycle in React Native is the same as in React: when props or state change, React Native re-renders the views. The major difference between React Native and React in the browser is that React Native does this by leveraging the UI libraries of its host platform, rather than using HTML and CSS markup.

For developers accustomed to working on the Web with React, this means you can write mobile apps with the performance and look and feel of a native application, while using familiar tools. React Native also represents an improvement over normal mobile development in two other areas: the developer experience and cross-platform development potential.

Developer Experience

If you've ever developed for mobile before, you might be surprised by how easy React Native is to work with. The React Native team has baked strong developer tools and meaningful error messages into the framework, so working with robust tools is a natural part of your development experience.

For instance, because React Native is "just" JavaScript, you don't need to rebuild your application in order to see your changes reflected; instead, you can hit Command+R to refresh your application just as you would any other web page. All of those minutes spent waiting for your application to build can really add up, and in contrast React Native's quick iteration cycle feels like a godsend.

Additionally, React Native lets you take advantage of intelligent debugging tools and error reporting. If you are comfortable with Chrome or Safari's developer tools (Figure 1-1), you will be happy to know that you can use them for mobile development, as well. Likewise, you can use whatever text editor you prefer for JavaScript editing: React Native does not force you to work in Xcode to develop for iOS, or Android Studio for Android development.

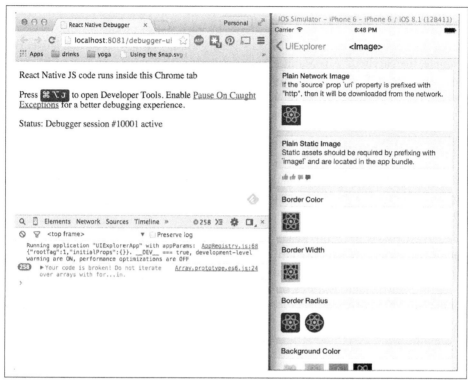

Figure 1-1. Using the Chrome Debugger

Besides the day-to-day improvements to your development experience, React Native also has the potential to positively impact your product release cycle. For instance, Apple permits JavaScript-based changes to an app's behavior to be loaded over the air with no additional review cycle necessary.

All of these small perks add up to saving you and your fellow developers time and energy, allowing you to focus on the more interesting parts of your work and be more productive overall.

Code Reuse and Knowledge Sharing

Working with React Native can dramatically shrink the resources required to build mobile applications. Any developer who knows how to write React code can now target the Web, iOS, and Android, all with the same skillset. By removing the need to "silo" developers based on their target platform, React Native lets your team iterate more quickly, and share knowledge and resources more effectively.

Besides shared knowledge, much of your code can be shared, too. Not *all* the code you write will be cross-platform, and depending on what functionality you need on a specific platform, you may occasionally need to dip into Objective-C or Java. (Happily, this isn't too bad, and we'll cover how so-called native modules work in Chapter 7.) But reusing code across platforms is surprisingly easy with React Native. For example, the Facebook Ads Manager application for Android shares 87% of its codebase with the iOS version, as noted in the React Europe 2015 keynote (*https://youtu.be/PAA9O4E1IM4*). The final application we'll look at in this book, a flashcard app, has total code reuse between Android and iOS. It's hard to beat that!

Risks and Drawbacks

As with anything, using React Native is not without its downsides, and whether or not React Native is a good fit for your team really depends on your individual situation.

The largest risk is probably React Native's maturity, as the project is still relatively young. iOS support was released in March 2015, and Android support was released in September 2015. The documentation certainly has room for improvement, and continues to evolve. Some features on iOS and Android still aren't supported, and the community is still discovering best practices. The good news is that in the vast majority of cases, you can implement support for missing APIs yourself, which we'll cover in Chapter 7.

Because React Native introduces another layer to your project, it can also make debugging hairier, especially at the intersection of React and the host platform. We'll cover debugging for React Native in more depth in Chapter 8, and try to address some of the most common issues.

React Native is still young, and the usual caveats that go along with working with new technologies apply here. Still, on the whole, I think you'll see that the benefits outweigh the risks.

Summary

React Native is an exciting framework that enables web developers to create robust mobile applications using their existing JavaScript knowledge. It offers faster mobile development, and more efficient code sharing across iOS, Android, and the Web, without sacrificing the end user's experience or application quality. The tradeoff is that it's new, and still a work in progress. If your team can handle the uncertainty that comes with working with a new technology, and wants to develop mobile applications for more than just one platform, you should be looking at React Native.

In the next chapter, we'll go over some of the main ways in which React Native differs from React for the Web, and cover some key concepts. If you'd like to skip straight to developing, feel free to jump to Chapter 3, in which we'll handle setting up our development environment and write our very first React Native application.

CHAPTER 2

Working with React Native

In this chapter, we'll cover the "bridge," and review how React Native works under the hood. Then, we'll look at how React Native components differ from their web counterparts, and cover what you'll need to know in order to create and style components for mobile.

 If you'd prefer to dig into the development process and see React Native in action, feel free to jump ahead to the next chapter!

How Does React Native Work?

The idea of writing mobile applications in JavaScript feels a little odd. How is it possible to use React in a mobile environment? In order to understand the technical underpinnings of React Native, first we'll need to recall one of React's features, the Virtual DOM.

In React, the Virtual DOM acts as a layer between the developer's description of how things ought to look, and the work done to actually render your application onto the page. To render interactive user interfaces in a browser, developers must edit the browser's DOM, or Document Object Model. This is an expensive step, and excessive writes to the DOM have a significant impact on performance. Rather than directly render changes on the page, React computes the necessary changes by using an in-memory version of the DOM, and rerenders the minimal amount necessary. Figure 2-1 shows how this works.

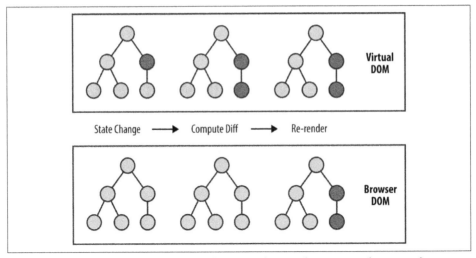

Figure 2-1. Performing calculations in the Virtual DOM limits rerendering in the Browser DOM

In the context of React on the Web, most developers think of the Virtual DOM primarily as a performance optimization. The Virtual DOM certainly has performance benefits, but its real potential lies in the power of its abstraction. Placing a clean abstraction layer between the developer's code and the actual rendering opens up a lot of interesting possibilities. What if React could render to a target other than the browser's DOM? After all, React already "understands" what your application is *supposed* to look like.

Indeed, this is how React Native works, as shown in Figure 2-2. Instead of rendering to the browser's DOM, React Native invokes Objective-C APIs to render to iOS components, or Java APIs to render to Android components. This sets React Native apart from other cross-platform app development options, which often end up rendering web-based views.

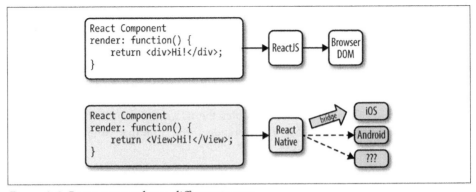

Figure 2-2. React can render to different targets

This is all possible because of the "bridge," which provides React with an interface into the host platform's native UI elements. React components return markup from their render function, which describes how they should look. With React for the Web, this translates directly to the browser's DOM. For React Native, this markup is translated to suit the host platform, so a <View> might become an iOS-specific UIView.

React Native currently supports iOS and Android. Because of the abstraction layer provided by the Virtual DOM, React Native could target other platforms, too—someone just needs to write the bridge.

Rendering Lifecycle

If you are accustomed to working in React, the React lifecycle should be familiar to you. When React runs in the browser, the render lifecycle begins by mounting your React components (Figure 2-3).

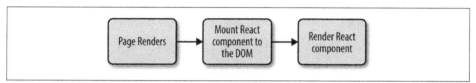

Figure 2-3. Mounting components in React

After that, React handles the rendering and rerendering of your component as necessary (Figure 2-4).

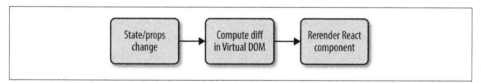

Figure 2-4. Rerendering components in React

For the render stage, the developer returns HTML markup from a React component's render method, which React then renders directly into the page as necessary.

For React Native, the lifecycle is the same, but the rendering process is slightly different, because React Native depends on the bridge. We looked at the bridge briefly earlier in Figure 2-2. The bridge translates JavaScript calls and invokes the host platform's underlying APIs and UI elements (i.e., in Objective-C or Java, as appropriate). Because React Native doesn't run on the main UI thread, it can perform these asynchronous calls without impacting the user's experience.

Creating Components in React Native

All React code lives in React components. React Native components are largely the same as ordinary React components, with some important differences around rendering and styling.

Working with Views

When writing in React for the Web, you render normal HTML elements (<div>, <p>, <span>, <a>, etc.). With React Native, all of these elements are replaced by platform-specific React components (see Table 2-1). The most basic is the cross-platform <View>, a simple and flexible UI element that can be thought of as analogous to the <div>. On iOS, for instance, the <View> component renders to a UIView, while on Android it renders to a View.

Table 2-1. Basic elements for the Web, compared with React Native

React	React Native
<div>	<View>
<span>	<Text>
<li>,<ul>	<ListView>
<img>	<Image>

Other components are platform-specific. For instance, the <DatePickerIOS> component (predictably) renders the iOS standard date picker. Here is an excerpt from the UIExplorer sample app, demonstrating an iOS date picker. The usage is straightforward, as you would expect:

```
<DatePickerIOS
  date={this.state.date}
  mode="date"
  timeZoneOffsetInMinutes={this.state.timeZoneOffsetInHours * 60}
/>
```

This renders to the standard iOS date picker (Figure 2-5).

January	15	2012
February	16	2013
March	17	2014
April	**18**	**2015**
May	19	2016
June	20	2017
July	21	2018

Figure 2-5. The DatePickerIOS is, as the name would suggest, iOS-specific

Because all of our UI elements are now React components, rather than basic HTML elements like the <div>, you will need to explicitly import each component you wish to use. For instance, we needed to import the <DatePickerIOS> component like so:

```
var React = require('react-native');
var {
  DatePickerIOS
} = React;
```

The UIExplorer application, which is bundled into the standard React Native examples (*https://github.com/facebook/react-native#examples*), allows you to view all of the supported UI elements. I encourage you to examine the various elements included in the UIExplorer app. It also demonstrates many styling options and interactions.

Platform-specific components and APIs have special tags in the documentation, and typically use the platform name as a suffix —for example, <SwitchAndroid> and <SwitchIOS>.

Because these components vary from platform to platform, how you structure your React components becomes even more important when working in React Native. In React for the Web, we often have a mix of React components: some manage logic and their child components, while other components render raw markup. If you want to reuse code when working in React Native, maintaining separation between these types of components becomes critical. A React component that renders a <DatePickerIOS> element obviously cannot be reused for Android. However, a component that encapsulates the associated *logic* can be reused. Then, the view component can be swapped out based on your platform. You can also designate platform-specific versions of components, if you want, so you can have a *picker.ios.js* and a *picker.android.js* file, for instance. We'll cover this in "Components with Platform-Specific Versions" on page 77.

Using JSX

In React Native, just as in React, we write our views using JSX, combining markup and the JavaScript that controls it into a single file. JSX met with strong reactions when React first debuted. For many web developers, the separation of files based on technologies is a given: you keep your CSS, HTML, and JavaScript files separate. The idea of combining markup, control logic, and even styling into one language can be confusing.

JSX prioritizes the separation of *concerns* over the separation of technologies. In React Native, this is even more strictly enforced. In a world without the browser, it makes even more sense to unify our styles, markup, and behavior in a single file for each component. Accordingly, your *.js* files in React Native are in fact JSX files. If you were using vanilla JavaScript when working with React for web, you will want to transition to JSX syntax for your work in React Native.

If you've never seen JSX before, don't worry: it's pretty simple. As an example, a pure-JavaScript React component for the Web might look something like this:

```
var HelloMessage = React.createClass({
  displayName: "HelloMessage",

  render: function render() {
    return React.createElement(
      "div",
      null,
      "Hello ",
      this.props.name
    );
  }
});
```

```
React.render(React.createElement(HelloMessage, { name: "Bonnie" }), mountNode);
```

We can render this more succinctly by using JSX. Instead of calling `React.createElement` and passing in a list of HTML attributes, we use XML-like markup:

```
var HelloMessage = React.createClass({
  render: function() {
    // Instead of calling createElement, we return markup
    return <div>Hello {this.props.name}</div>;
  }
});

// We no longer need a createElement call here
React.render(<HelloMessage name="Bonnie" />, mountNode);
```

Both of these will render the following HTML onto the page:

```
<div>Hello Bonnie</div>
```

Styling Native Components

On the Web, we style React components using CSS, just as we would any other HTML element. Whether you love it or hate it, CSS is a necessary part of the Web. React usually does not affect the way we write CSS. It does make it easier to use (sane, useful) inline styles, and to dynamically build class names based on props and state, but otherwise React is mostly agnostic about how we handle styles on the Web.

Non-web platforms have a wide array of approaches to layout and styling. When we work with React Native, thankfully, we utilize one standardized approach to styling. Part of the bridge between React and the host platform includes the implementation of a heavily pruned subset of CSS. This narrow implementation of CSS relies primarily on flexbox for layout, and focuses on simplicity rather than implementing the full range of CSS rules. Unlike the Web, where CSS support varies across browsers, React Native is able to enforce consistent support of style rules. Much like the various UI elements, you can see many examples of supported styles in the UIExplorer (*http:// bit.ly/1MXpGlK*) application, which is one of the examples that ships with React Native.

React Native also insists on the use of inline styles, which exist as JavaScript objects. The React team has advocated for this approach before in React for web applications. If you have previously experimented with inline styles in React, the syntax will look familiar to you:

```
// Define a style...
var style = {
  backgroundColor: 'white',
  fontSize: '16px'
};

// ...and then apply it.
var tv = (
  <Text style={style}>
    A styled Text
  </Text>);
```

React Native also provides us with some utilities for creating and extending style objects that make dealing with inline styles a more manageable process. We will explore those later, in Chapter 5.

Does looking at inline styles make you twitch? Coming from a web-based background, this is admittedly a break from standard practices. Working with style objects, as opposed to stylesheets, takes some mental adjustments, and changes the way you need to approach writing styles. However, in the context of React Native, it is a useful shift. We will be discussing styling best practices and workflow later on, in Chapter 5. Just try not to be surprised when you see them in use!

Host Platform APIs

Perhaps the biggest difference between React for the Web and React Native is the way we think about host platform APIs. On the Web, the issue at hand is often fragmented and inconsistent adoption of standards; still, most browsers support a common core of shared features. With React Native, however, platform-specific APIs play a much larger role in creating an excellent, natural-feeling user experience. There are also many more options to consider. Mobile APIs include everything from data storage, to location services, to accessing hardware such as the camera. As React Native expands to other platforms, we can expect to see other sorts of APIs, too; what would the interface look like between React Native and a virtual reality headset, for instance?

By default, React Native for iOS and Android includes support for many of the commonly used features, and React Native can support any asynchronous native API. We will take a look at many of them throughout this book. React Native makes it straightforward and simple to make use of host platform APIs, so you can experiment freely. Be sure to think about what feels "right" for your target platform, and design with natural interactions in mind.

Inevitably, the React Native bridge will not expose all host platform functionality. If you find yourself in need of an unsupported feature, you have the option of adding it to React Native yourself. Alternatively, chances are good that someone else has done so already, so be sure to check in with the community to see whether or not support will be forthcoming. We'll cover this in Chapter 7.

Also worth noting is that utilizing host platform APIs has implications for code reuse. React components that need platform-specific functionality will be platform-specific as well. Isolating and encapsulating those components will bring added flexibility to your application. Of course, this applies for the Web, too: if you plan on sharing code between React Native and React, keep in mind that things like the DOM do not actually exist in React Native.

Summary

Writing components for mobile is a bit different in React Native when compared with React for the Web. JSX is mandatory, and our basic building blocks are now components such as <View> in lieu of HTML elements such as <div>. Styling is also quite different, based on a subset of CSS, and we assign styles with inline syntax. Still, these adjustments are quite manageable. In the next chapter, we'll put this into practice as we build our first application!

CHAPTER 3

Building Your First Application

In this chapter, we will cover how to set up your local development environment for working with React Native. Then, we will go through the basics of creating a simple application, which you will then be able to deploy to your own iOS or Android device.

Setting Up Your Environment

Setting up your development environment will enable you to follow along with the examples in the book, and will let you write your own applications!

Instructions for installing React Native can be found in the official React Native documentation (*http://facebook.github.io/react-native/*). The official site will be your most up-to-date reference point for specific installation steps, but we'll walk through them here as well.

You will need to use Homebrew (*http://brew.sh/*), a common package manager for OS X, in order to install React Native's dependencies. Throughout this book, we will assume that you are developing on OS X, which allows you to write both iOS and Android applications.

Once you have Homebrew installed, run the following from the command line:

```
brew install node
brew install watchman
brew install flow
```

The React Native packager uses both node and watchman, so if the packager gives you trouble in the future it's worth updating these dependencies. flow is Facebook's type-checking library, and is also used by React Native. (If you want to enable type-checking in your React Native projects, you can use flow!)

If you encounter difficulties, you may need to update brew and upgrade any packages (note that these commands may take a little while to run):

```
brew update
brew upgrade
```

If you see errors after doing so, you'll need to fix your local brew setup. brew doctor can point you to probable issues.

Installing React Native

Now that you have node installed, you can use npm (the Node Package Manager) to install the React Native command-line tools:

```
npm install -g react-native-cli
```

This installs the React Native command-line tools globally on your system. After this is done, congrats; React Native is installed!

Next, you'll have to handle the platform-specific setup. In order to develop for a given mobile platform, you will need to install that platform's development dependencies. To continue on with this chapter, you can choose iOS, Android, or both.

iOS Dependencies

In order to develop and release apps for iOS, you will need to acquire an iOS developer's account. The account is free, and is sufficient for development. For deploying applications to the iOS App Store, you'll eventually need a license, which is priced at $99/year.

If you haven't done so already, you'll want to download and install Xcode, which includes the Xcode IDE, the iOS simulators, and the iOS SDK. You can download Xcode from the App Store or from the Xcode website (*https://developer.apple.com/xcode/download/*).

After Xcode is installed, accept the license, and you should be good to go.

Android Dependencies

Android setup is a multistep process. You should check the official documentation (*https://facebook.github.io/react-native/docs/android-setup.html*) for the most up-to-date instructions. Note that these instructions assume you don't already have your environment setup for Android development. In general terms, there are three main phases: installing the SDKs, installing the simulator tools, and creating simulators for use.

First, you'll need to install the JDK (Java Development Kit) and Android SDKs:

1. Install the latest JDK (*http://bit.ly/1X9h0Ea*).

2. Install the Android SDK, using **brew install android-sdk**.

3. Export your `ANDROID_HOME` variable appropriately in your shell config file (*~/.bashrc, ~/.zshrc*, or whichever your shell uses):

```
export ANDROID_HOME=/usr/local/opt/android-sdk
```

This environment variable is used for many Android-related development tasks; make sure to source your shell config after adding it.

Next, run **android** from the command line to open the Android SDK Manager. This will show you the available packages that you can install (see Figure 3-1).

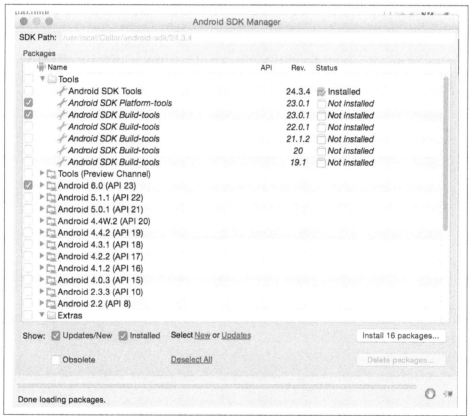

Figure 3-1. The Android SDK Manager allows you to choose which packages to install

Wait for the SDK Manager to update and download the package listing. Some packages will already be checked by default. Also make sure to check the boxes for:

- Android SDK Build-tools version 23.0.1
- Android 6.0 (API 23)
- Android Support Repository

Then, click Install Packages and accept any applicable licenses. It'll take a little while for everything to install.

Next, you'll want to install the simulator and related tools.

Start a new shell and run `android` again to launch the Android SDK Manager. We're going to install a few more packages:

- Intel x86 Atom System Image (for Android 5.1.1–API 22)
- Intel x86 Emulator Accelerator (HAXM installer)

Once again, click Install Packages and accept any applicable licenses.

These packages give us the ability to create Android Virtual Devices (AVDs), or emulators, but we don't actually have any emulators created yet. Let's correct that. Launch the AVD Manager (shown in Figure 3-2) by running:

```
android avd
```

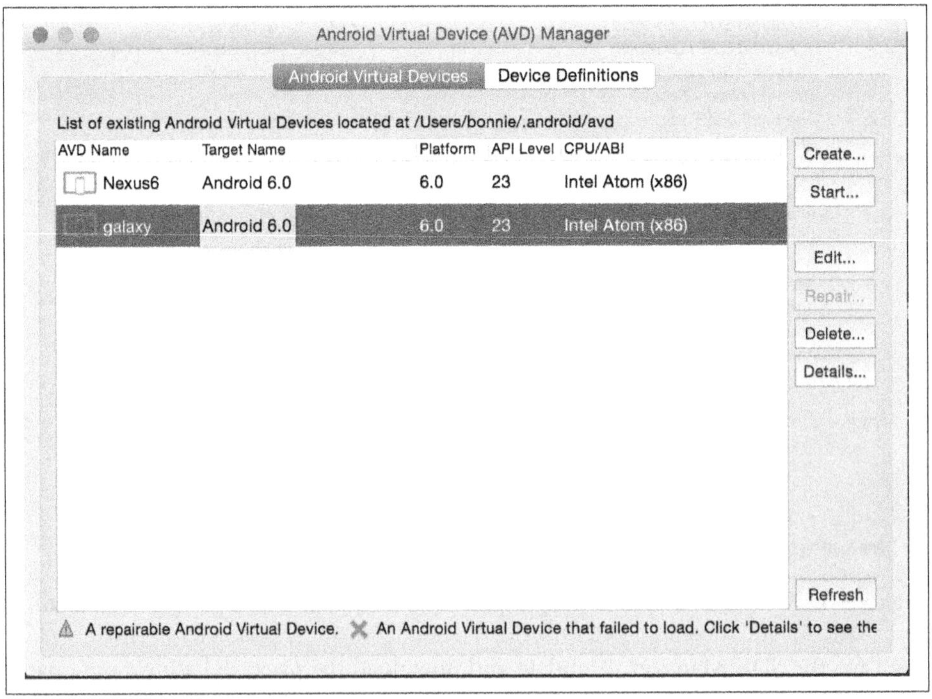

Figure 3-2. The AVD manager lets you create and launch emulators

---

Then, click Create… and fill out the emulator creation form, shown in Figure 3-3. For Emulation Options, be sure to check Use Host GPU (see Figure 3-4).

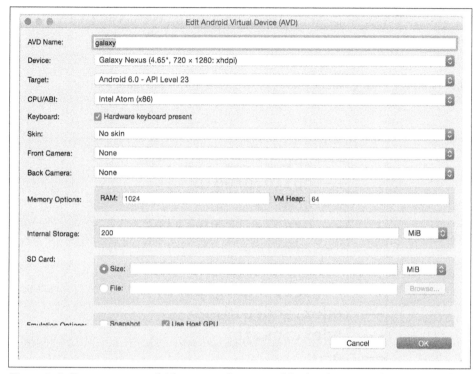

Figure 3-3. *You can create whichever emulators you like (in this example, I've created a Galaxy Nexus emulator)*

Figure 3-4. *Be sure to check Use Host GPU—otherwise your emulator will be very slow!*

You can create as many AVDs as you like. Because Android devices vary so much—in screen size, resolution, and capabilities—having multiple emulators to use for testing is often helpful. To get started, though, we just need one.

Creating a New Application

You can use the React Native command-line tools to create a new application. This will generate a fresh project with all of the React Native, iOS, and Android boilerplate for you:

```
react-native init FirstProject
```

The resulting directory should have the structure shown in Figure 3-5.

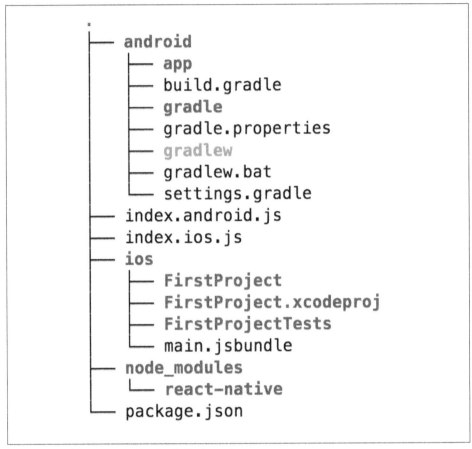

```
.
├── android
│   ├── app
│   ├── build.gradle
│   ├── gradle
│   ├── gradle.properties
│   ├── gradlew
│   ├── gradlew.bat
│   └── settings.gradle
├── index.android.js
├── index.ios.js
├── ios
│   ├── FirstProject
│   ├── FirstProject.xcodeproj
│   ├── FirstProjectTests
│   └── main.jsbundle
├── node_modules
│   └── react-native
└── package.json
```

Figure 3-5. File structure in the default project

The *ios/* and *android/* directories contain boilerplate relevant to those platforms. Your React code is located in the *index.ios.js* and *android.ios.js* files, which are the respective entry points for your React application. Dependencies installed via npm can, as usual, be found in the *node_modules/* folder.

If you would prefer, you can download the project from the GitHub repository (*https://github.com/bonniee/learning-react-native*) for this book.

Running a React Native Application for iOS

For starters, we'll try running the iOS version of our React Native application, both in the simulator and on a physical device.

Open the *FirstProject.xcodeproj* file, located in the *ios/* directory, in Xcode. In the top left, you'll notice a Run button, as shown in Figure 3-6. Pressing this will build and run your application. You can also change the deploy target here to a different iOS simulator.

Figure 3-6. The Run button, with deploy target selector

When you press Run, the React packager should automatically launch in a new terminal window. If it fails to launch, or prints an error, try running npm install and npm start from the *FirstProject/* directory.

It should look like the screenshot shown in Figure 3-7.

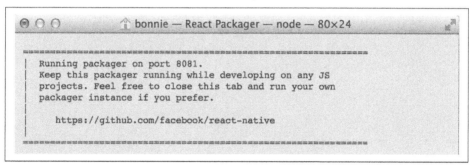

Figure 3-7. The React packager

Once the packager is ready, the iOS simulator will launch with the default application. It should look something like Figure 3-8.

Figure 3-8. Screenshot of the default app

You need the packager running at all times while developing in order to have changes in your code reflected in the app. If the packager crashes, you can restart it by navigating to your project's directory and running `npm start`.

Uploading to Your iOS Device

To upload your React Native application to a physical iOS device, you will need an iOS developer account with Apple. You will then need to generate a certificate and register your device. After registering with Apple, open Xcode's preferences and add your account, as shown in Figure 3-9.

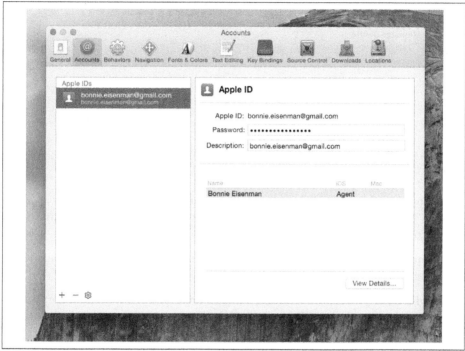

Figure 3-9. Add your account in Xcode's Preferences pane

Next, you will need to obtain a certificate for your account. The easiest way to do this is to check the General pane in Xcode. As shown in Figure 3-10, you will notice a warning symbol. Click on the Fix Issue button to resolve this problem. Xcode should walk you through the next few steps required in order to get a certificate from Apple.

Figure 3-10. Screenshot of the default app

Having obtained a certificate, you're nearly done. The final step is to log on to Apple Developer (*http://developer.apple.com*) and register your device (see Figure 3-11).

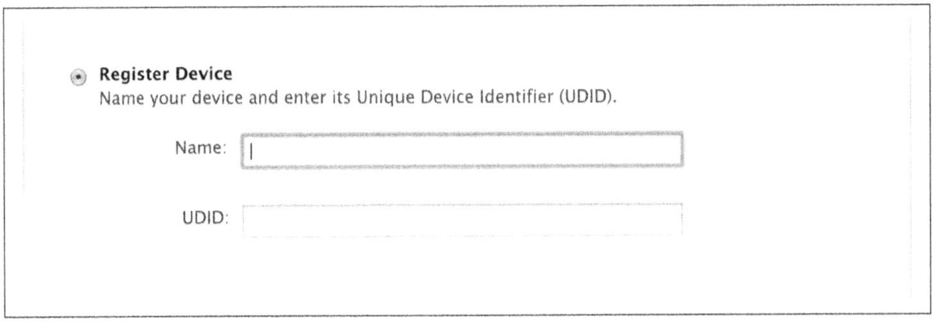

Figure 3-11. Registering your device in the iOS developer member center

Obtaining your device's UDID is simple. Open iTunes, and select your device. Then, click on the serial number; it should now display the UDID instead, and the UDID will be copied over to your clipboard.

Once you have registered your device with Apple, it should appear in your list of approved devices.

This registration process can also be used later on, if you wish to distribute an early release to other test devices. For individual developers, Apple gives you an allotment of 100 devices per year through the developer program.

Lastly, we need to make a quick change to our code before we can deploy. You will need to alter your *AppDelegate.m* file to include your Mac's IP address instead of localhost. If you do not know how to find your computer's IP address, you can run **ifconfig** and then use the inet value under en0.

For example, if your IP address was 10.10.12.345, you should edit the jsCodeLocation to look like this:

```
jsCodeLocation =
[NSURL URLWithString:@"http://10.10.12.345:8081/index.ios.bundle"];
```

Phew! With all of that out of the way, we can select a physical device as the deploy target in Xcode (see Figure 3-12).

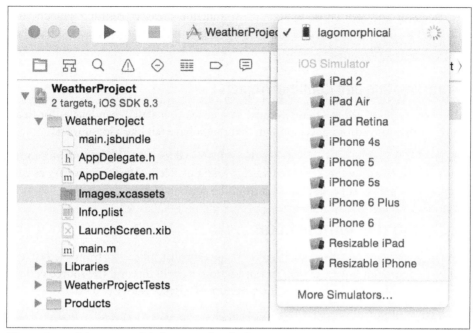

Figure 3-12. Select your iOS device as the deploy target

Once that is done, click the Run button. The app should load onto your device, just as it did in the simulator! If you close the app, you will see that it's been loaded onto your home screen, too.

Running a React Native Application for Android

To run a React Native application for Android, you'll need to do two things: start the emulator, and then run your application.

Earlier, in Figure 3-2, we saw that we can launch the AVD Manager by running:

```
android avd
```

Select the emulator you would like to run and then click the Start… button

Alternatively, you can launch your emulators from the command line. To view available emulators, type:

```
emulator -list-avds
```

Then launch them by name, prefixed by the @ symbol. For instance, I have an AVD named "galaxy," so I can run the following:

```
emulator @galaxy
```

Regardless of how you chose to start your emulator, once it's running, launch your React Native application by running the following from your project's root directory:

```
react-native run-android
```

Recap: Creating and Running Projects

We covered a lot of ground here! Because we needed to install dependencies for React Native, iOS, and Android development, that might have felt like a lot of work.

The good news is that now that you've done the initial legwork, things will be simpler in the future. Creating the React Native equivalent of "Hello, World" is as easy as running `react-native init HelloWorld` from the command line.

Exploring the Sample Code

Now that you have launched and deployed the default application from the last section, let's figure out how it works. In this section, we will dig into the source code of the default application and explore the structure of a React Native project.

Attaching a Component to the View

When a React Native application launches, how does a React component get bound to the view? What determines which component is rendered?

This answer is platform-specific. We'll start by looking at the iOS version of our project.

We can find the answer inside of *AppDelegate.m*. Notice, in particular, the lines shown in Example 3-1.

Example 3-1. Declaring the root view in ios/AppDelegate.m

```
RCTRootView *rootView =
  [[RCTRootView alloc] initWithBundleURL:jsCodeLocation
  moduleName:@"FirstProject"
  launchOptions:launchOptions];
```

The React Native library prefixes all of its classes with RCT, meaning that RCTRootView is a React Native class. In this case, the RCTRootView represents the root React view. The remainder of the boilerplate code in *AppDelegate.m* handles attaching this view to a UIViewController and rendering the view to the screen. These steps are analogous to mounting a React component to a DOM node with a call to React.render.

For now, the *AppDelegate.m* file contains two things that you ought to know how to modify.

The first is the `jsCodeLocation` line, which we edited earlier in order to deploy to a physical device. As the comments in the generated file explain, the first option is used for development, while the second option is used for deploying with a prebundled file on disk. For now, we will leave the first option uncommented. Later, once we prepare to deploy applications to the App Store, we will discuss these two approaches in more detail.

You'll also need to modify the `moduleName`, which is passed to the `RCTRootView` and determines which component will be mounted in the view. This is where you can choose which component should be rendered by your application.

In order to use the `FirstProject` component here, you need to register a React component with the same name. If you open up *index.ios.js*, you'll see that this is accomplished on the last line (Example 3-2).

Example 3-2. Registering the top-level component

```
AppRegistry.registerComponent('FirstProject', () => FirstProject);
```

This exposes the FirstProject component so that we can use it in *AppDelegate.m*. For the most part, you will not need to modify this boilerplate, but it's good to know that it's there.

What about on Android? The story is pretty similar. If you look at *MainActivity.java*, you'll notice the line shown in Example 3-3.

Example 3-3. React entry point for Android is in MainActivity.java

```
mReactRootView.startReactApplication(mReactInstanceManager, "FirstProject", null);
```

Like *AppDelegate.m* for iOS, the *MainActivity.java* file for Android will look to the `AppRegistry` for a React component bound to the name `FirstProject`.

Imports in React Native

Let's take a closer look at the *index.ios.js* file. As you can see in Example 3-4, the `require` statements used are a bit different than normal.

Example 3-4. require statements in React Native, and importing UI elements

```
var React = require('react-native');
var {
  AppRegistry,
  StyleSheet,
  Text,
  View,
} = React;
```

There's some interesting syntax going on here. React is required as usual, but what is happening on the next line?

One quirk of working with React Native is that you need to explicitly require every Native-provided module you work with. Things like <div> don't simply exist; instead, you need to explicitly import components such as <View> and <Text>. Library functions such as Stylesheet and AppRegistry are also explicitly imported using this syntax. Once we start building our own applications, we will explore the other React Native functions that you may need to import.

If the syntax is unfamiliar to you, check out Example A-2 in Appendix A for an explanation of destructuring in ES6.

The FirstProject Component

Let's take a look at the <FirstProject> component (Example 3-5), which is duplicated between *index.ios.js* and *index.android.js* (in other words, you can examine either, as they're identical).

This should all look comfortably familiar, because <FirstProject> is written just like an ordinary React component. The main difference is its use of <Text> and <View> components instead of <div> and <span>, and the use of style objects.

Example 3-5. FirstProject component, with styles

```
var FirstProject = React.createClass({
  render: function() {
    return (
      <View style={styles.container}>
        <Text style={styles.welcome}>
          Welcome to React Native!
        </Text>
        <Text style={styles.instructions}>
          To get started, edit index.ios.js
        </Text>
        <Text style={styles.instructions}>
          Press Cmd+R to reload,{'\n'}
          Cmd+D or shake for dev menu
        </Text>
      </View>
    );
  }
});

var styles = StyleSheet.create({
  container: {
    flex: 1,
    justifyContent: 'center',
    alignItems: 'center',
```

```
    backgroundColor: '#F5FCFF',
  },
  welcome: {
    fontSize: 20,
    textAlign: 'center',
    margin: 10,
  },
  instructions: {
    textAlign: 'center',
    color: '#333333',
    marginBottom: 5,
  },
});
```

As I mentioned earlier, all styling in React Native is done with style objects rather than stylesheets. The standard method of doing this is by utilizing the `StyleSheet` library. You can see how the style objects are defined toward the bottom of the file. Note that only `<Text>` components can take text-specific styles like `fontSize`, and that all layout logic is handled by flexbox. We will discuss how to build layouts with flexbox at greater length later on in Chapter 5.

The sample application is a good demonstration of the basic functions you will need to create React Native applications. It mounts a React component for rendering, and demonstrates the basics of styling and rendering in React Native. It also gave us a simple way to test our development setup, and try deploying to a real device. However, it's still a very basic application, with no user interaction. Let's try building a more full-featured application.

Building a Weather App

We will be building off of the sample application to create a weather app (you can create a new one for this example with **react-native init WeatherProject**). This will give us a chance to explore how to utilize and combine stylesheets, flexbox, network communication, user input, and images into a useful app we can then deploy to an Android or iOS device.

This section may feel like a bit of a blur, as we'll be focusing on an overview of these features rather than deep explanations of them. The Weather App will serve as a useful reference in future sections as we discuss these features in more detail. Don't worry if it feels like we're moving quickly!

As shown in Figure 3-13, the final application includes a text field where users can input a zip code. It will then fetch data from the OpenWeatherMap API and display the current weather.

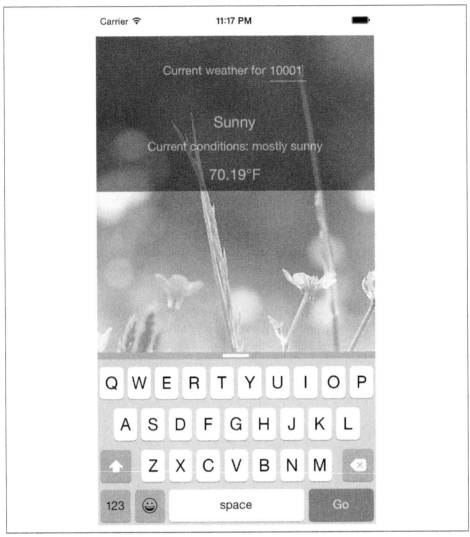

Figure 3-13. The finished weather app

The first thing we'll do is replace the default code. Move the initial component out into its own file, *WeatherProject.js*, and replace the contents of *index.ios.js* and *index.android.js*.

Example 3-6. Simplified contents of index.ios.js and index.android.js (they should be identical)

```
var React = require('react-native');
var { AppRegistry } = React;
```

```
var WeatherProject = require('./WeatherProject');
AppRegistry.registerComponent('WeatherProject', () => WeatherProject);
```

Handling User Input

We want the user to be able to input a zip code and get the forecast for that area, so we need to add a text field for user input. We can start by adding zip code information to our component's initial state (see Example 3-7).

Example 3-7. Add this to your component, before the render function

```
getInitialState: function() {
  return {
    zip: ''
  };
}
```

Remember that `getInitialState` is how we set up the initial `state` values for React components. If you need a review of the React component lifecycle, see the React docs (*https://facebook.github.io/react/docs/component-specs.html*).

Then, we should also change one of the `<Text>` components to display `this.state.zip`:

```
<Text style={styles.welcome}>
  You input {this.state.zip}.
</Text>
```

With that out of the way, let's add a `<TextInput>` component (this is a basic component that allows the user to enter text):

```
<TextInput
  style={styles.input}
  onSubmitEditing={this._handleTextChange}/>
```

The `<TextInput>` component is documented on the React Native site (*http://bit.ly/1N6vHN5*), along with its properties. You can also pass the `<TextInput>` additional callbacks in order to listen to other events, such as `onChange` or `onFocus`, but we do not need them at the moment.

Note that we've added a simple style to the `<TextInput>`. Add the input style to your stylesheet:

```
var styles = StyleSheet.create({
  ...
  input: {
    fontSize: 20,
    borderWidth: 2,
    height: 40
    }
```

```
  . . .
});
```

The callback we passed as the onSubmitEditing prop looks like this, and should be added as a function on the component:

```
_handleTextChange(event) {
  console.log(event.nativeEvent.text);
  this.setState({zip: event.nativeEvent.text})
}
```

The console statement is extraneous, but it will allow you to test out the debugger tools if you so desire.

You will also need to update your import statements:

```
var React = require('react-native');
var {
  . . .
  TextInput
  . . .
} = React;
```

Now, try running your application using the iOS simulator. It won't be pretty, but you should be able to successfully submit a zip code and have it be reflected in the <Text> component.

If we wanted, we could add some simple input validation here to ensure that the user typed in a five-digit number, but we will skip that for now.

Example 3-8 shows the full code for the *WeatherProject.js* component.

Example 3-8. WeatherProject.js: this version simply accepts and records user input

```
var React = require('react-native');
var {
  StyleSheet,
  Text,
  View,
  TextInput,
  Image
} = React;


var WeatherProject = React.createClass({
  // If you want to have a default zip code, you could add one here
  getInitialState() {
    return ({
      zip: ''
    });
  },
  // We'll pass this callback to the <TextInput>
```

```
  _handleTextChange(event) {

    // log statements are viewable in Xcode,
    // or the Chrome debug tools
    console.log(event.nativeEvent.text);

    this.setState({
      zip: event.nativeEvent.text
    });
  },
  render() {
    return (
      <View style={styles.container}>
        <Text style={styles.welcome}>
          You input {this.state.zip}.
        </Text>
        <TextInput
              style={styles.input}
              onSubmitEditing={this._handleTextChange}/>
      </View>
    );
  }
});

var styles = StyleSheet.create({
  container: {
    flex: 1,
    justifyContent: 'center',
    alignItems: 'center',
    backgroundColor: '#F5FCFF',
  },
  welcome: {
    fontSize: 20,
    textAlign: 'center',
    margin: 10,
  },
  input: {
    fontSize: 20,
    borderWidth: 2,
    height: 40
    }
});

module.exports = WeatherProject;
```

Displaying Data

Now let's work on displaying the forecast for that zip code. We will start by adding some mock data to `getInitialState` in *WeatherProject.js*:

```
getInitialState() {
  return {
```

```
          zip: '',
          forecast: {
            main: 'Clouds',
            description: 'few clouds',
            temp: 45.7
          }
        }
      }
```

For sanity's sake, let's also pull the forecast rendering into its own component. Make a new file called *Forecast.js* (see Example 3-9).

Example 3-9. Forecast component in Forecast.js

```
var React = require('react-native');
var {
  StyleSheet,
  Text,
  View
} = React;

var Forecast = React.createClass({
  render: function() {
    return (
      <View>
        <Text style={styles.bigText}>
          {this.props.main}
        </Text>
        <Text style={styles.mainText}>
          Current conditions: {this.props.description}
        </Text>
        <Text style={styles.bigText}>
          {this.props.temp}°F
        </Text>
      </View>
    );
  }
});


var styles = StyleSheet.create({
  bigText: {
    flex: 2,
    fontSize: 20,
    textAlign: 'center',
    margin: 10,
    color: '#FFFFFF'
  },
  mainText: {
    flex: 1,
    fontSize: 16,
    textAlign: 'center',
```

```
    color: '#FFFFFF'
  }
})

module.exports = Forecast;
```

The <Forecast> component just renders some <Text> based on its props. We've also included some simple styles at the bottom of the file, to control things like text color.

Require the <Forecast> component and then add it to your app's render method, passing it props based on the this.state.forecast (see Example 3-10). We'll address issues with layout and styling later. You can see how the <Forecast> component appears in the resulting application in Figure 3-14.

Example 3-10. WeatherProject.js should be updated with new state and the Forecast component

```
var React = require('react-native');
var {
  StyleSheet,
  Text,
  View,
  TextInput,
  Image
} = React;

var Forecast = require('./Forecast');

var WeatherProject = React.createClass({
  getInitialState() {
    return {
      zip: '',
      forecast: {
        main: 'Clouds',
        description: 'few clouds',
        temp: 45.7
      }
    }
  },
  _handleTextChange(event) {
    console.log(event.nativeEvent.text);
    this.setState({
      zip: event.nativeEvent.text
    });
  },
  render() {
    return (
      <View style={styles.container}>
        <Text style={styles.welcome}>
          You input {this.state.zip}.
        </Text>
```

```
      <Forecast
        main={this.state.forecast.main}
        description={this.state.forecast.description}
        temp={this.state.forecast.temp}/>
      <TextInput
        style={styles.input}
        returnKeyType='go'
        onSubmitEditing={this._handleTextChange}/>
    </View>
  );
  }
});

var styles = StyleSheet.create({
  container: {
    flex: 1,
    justifyContent: 'center',
    alignItems: 'center',
    backgroundColor: '#4D4D4D',
  },
  welcome: {
    fontSize: 20,
    textAlign: 'center',
    margin: 10,
  },
  input: {
    fontSize: 20,
    borderWidth: 2,
    height: 40
    }
});

module.exports = WeatherProject;
```

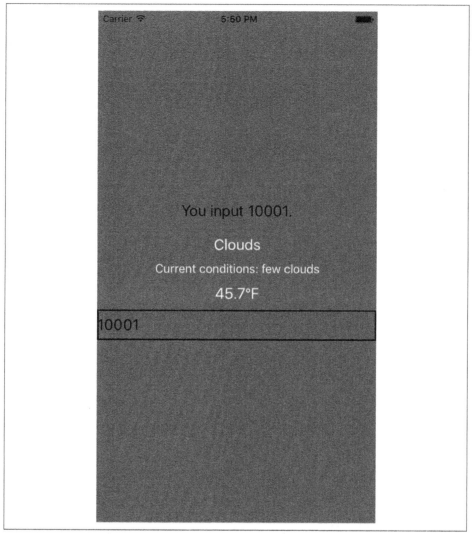

Carrier 🛜   5:50 PM

You input 10001.

Clouds

Current conditions: few clouds

45.7°F

10001

Figure 3-14. The weather app so far

Adding a Background Image

Plain background colors are boring. Let's display a background image to go along with our forecast.

Asset Inclusion Is Platform-Specific

Android and iOS have different requirements for adding assets to your projects. We'll cover both here.

Assets such as images need to be added to your project based on which platform you're building for. We'll start with Xcode.

Select the *Images.xcassets/* folder, and then select the New Image Set option, as shown in Figure 3-15. Then, you can drag and drop an image into the set. Figure 3-16 shows the resulting Image Set. Make sure the image set's name matches the filename, otherwise React Native will have difficulty importing it.

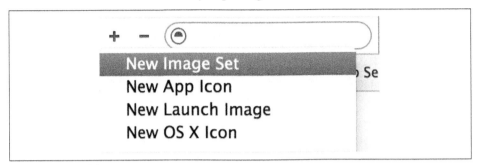

Figure 3-15. Add a new image set

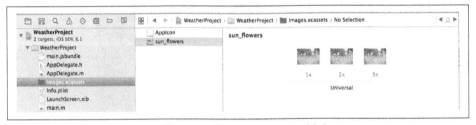

Figure 3-16. Drag your image files into the image set to add them

The @2x and @3x decorators indicate an image with a resolution of twice and thrice the base resolution, respectively. Because the WeatherApp is designated as a universal application (meaning one that can run on iPhone or iPad), Xcode gives us the option of uploading images at the various appropriate resolutions.

For Android, we have to add our files as bitmap drawable resources (*http://bit.ly/ 1N93oSC*) to the appropriate folders in *WeatherProject/android/app/src/main/res.* You'll want to copy the *.png* file into the following resolution-specific directories (see Figure 3-17):

- *drawable-mdpi/* (1x)
- *drawable-hdpi/* (1.5x)
- *drawable-xhdpi/* (2x)
- *drawable-xxhdpi/* (3x)

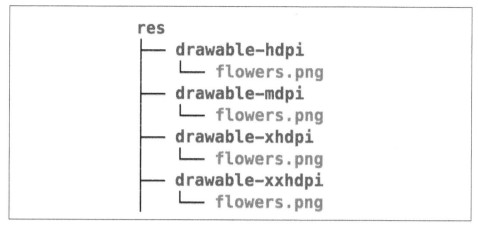

```
res
├── drawable-hdpi
│       └── flowers.png
├── drawable-mdpi
│       └── flowers.png
├── drawable-xhdpi
│       └── flowers.png
├── drawable-xxhdpi
│       └── flowers.png
```

Figure 3-17. Adding image files to Android

After that, the image will be available to your Android application.

If this workflow feels suboptimal, that's because it is. It will probably change in future versions of React Native.

Now that the image files have been imported into both our Android and iOS projects, let's hop back to our React code. To add a background image, we don't set a background property on a <div> like we can do on the Web. Instead, we use an <Image> component as a container:

```
<Image source={require('image!flowers')}
       resizeMode='cover'
       style={styles.backdrop}>
  // Your content here
</Image>
```

The <Image> component expects a source prop, which we get by using require. The call to require(image!flowers) will cause React Native to search for a file named *flowers*.

Don't forget to style it with flexDirection so that its children render as we'd like them to:

```
backdrop: {
  flex: 1,
  flexDirection: 'column'
}
```

Now let's give the <Image> some children. Update the render method of the <Weather Project> component to return the following:

```
<Image source={require('image!flowers')}
       resizeMode='cover'
```

```
        style={styles.backdrop}>
  <View style={styles.overlay}>
   <View style={styles.row}>
     <Text style={styles.mainText}>
       Current weather for
     </Text>
     <View style={styles.zipContainer}>
       <TextInput
         style={[styles.zipCode, styles.mainText]}
         returnKeyType='go'
         onSubmitEditing={this._handleTextChange}/>
     </View>
   </View>
   <Forecast
      main={this.state.forecast.main}
      description={this.state.forecast.description}
      temp={this.state.forecast.temp}/>
  </View>
</Image>
```

You'll notice that I'm using some additional styles that we haven't discussed yet, such as row, overlay, and the zipContainer and zipCode styles. You can skip ahead to the end of this section to see the full stylesheet.

Fetching Data from the Web

Next, let's explore using the networking APIs available in React Native. You won't be using jQuery to send AJAX requests from mobile devices! Instead, React Native implements the Fetch API. The Promise-based syntax is fairly simple:

```
fetch('http://www.somesite.com')
  .then((response) => response.text())
  .then((responseText) => {
    console.log(responseText);
  });
```

We will be using the OpenWeatherMap API, which provides us with a simple endpoint that returns the current weather for a given zip code.

To integrate this API, we can change the callback on the <TextInput> component to query the OpenWeatherMap API:

```
_handleTextChange: function(event) {
  var zip = event.nativeEvent.text;
  this.setState({zip: zip});
  fetch('http://api.openweathermap.org/data/2.5/weather?q=' +
  zip + '&units=imperial')
    .then((response) => response.json())
    .then((responseJSON) => {
      // Take a look at the format, if you want.
      console.log(responseJSON);
      this.setState({
```

```
      forecast: {
        main: responseJSON.weather[0].main,
        description: responseJSON.weather[0].description,
        temp: responseJSON.main.temp
      }
    });
  })
  .catch((error) => {
    console.warn(error);
  });
}
```

Note that we want the JSON from the response. The Fetch API is pretty straightforward to work with, so this is all we will need to do.

The other thing that we can do is to remove the placeholder data, and make sure that the forecast does not render if we do not have data yet.

First, clear the mock data from `getInitialState`:

```
getInitialState: function() {
  return {
    zip: '',
    forecast: null
  };
}
```

Then, in the render function, update the rendering logic:

```
var content = null;
if (this.state.forecast !== null) {
  content = <Forecast
            main={this.state.forecast.main}
            description={this.state.forecast.description}
            temp={this.state.forecast.temp}/>;
}
```

Finally, replace your rendered `<Forecast>` component with `{content}` in the render function.

Putting It Together

For the final version of the application, I've reorganized the `<WeatherProject>` component's `render` function and tweaked the styles. The main change is to the layout logic, diagrammed in Figure 3-18.

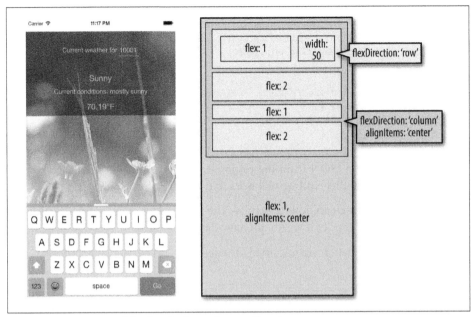

Figure 3-18. Layout of the finished weather application

OK. Ready to see it all in one place? Example 3-11 shows the finished code for the
`<WeatherProject>` component in full, including the stylesheets. The `<Forecast>`
component will be the same as above in Example 3-9.

Example 3-11. Finished code for WeatherProject.js

```
var React = require('react-native');
var {
  StyleSheet,
  Text,
  View,
  TextInput,
  Image
} = React;
var Forecast = require('./Forecast');

var WeatherProject = React.createClass({
  getInitialState: function() {
    return {
      zip: '',
      forecast: null
    };
  },

  _handleTextChange: function(event) {
    var zip = event.nativeEvent.text;
```

```
      this.setState({zip: zip});
      fetch('http://api.openweathermap.org/data/2.5/weather?q='
        + zip + '&units=imperial')
        .then((response) => response.json())
        .then((responseJSON) => {
          this.setState({
            forecast: {
              main: responseJSON.weather[0].main,
              description: responseJSON.weather[0].description,
              temp: responseJSON.main.temp
            }
          });
        })
        .catch((error) => {
          console.warn(error);
        });
    },

    render: function() {
      var content = null;
      if (this.state.forecast !== null) {
        content = <Forecast
                    main={this.state.forecast.main}
                    description={this.state.forecast.description}
                    temp={this.state.forecast.temp}/>;
      }
      return (
        <View style={styles.container}>
          <Image source={require('image!flowers')}
                 resizeMode='cover'
                 style={styles.backdrop}>
            <View style={styles.overlay}>
             <View style={styles.row}>
               <Text style={styles.mainText}>
                 Current weather for
               </Text>
               <View style={styles.zipContainer}>
                 <TextInput
                   style={[styles.zipCode, styles.mainText]}
                   returnKeyType='go'
                   onSubmitEditing={this._handleTextChange}/>
               </View>
             </View>
             {content}
            </View>
          </Image>
        </View>
      );
    }
});

var baseFontSize = 16;
```

```
var styles = StyleSheet.create({
  container: {
    flex: 1,
    alignItems: 'center',
    paddingTop: 30
  },
  backdrop: {
    flex: 1,
    flexDirection: 'column'
  },
  overlay: {
    paddingTop: 5,
    backgroundColor: '#000000',
    opacity: 0.5,
    flexDirection: 'column',
    alignItems: 'center'
  },
  row: {
    flex: 1,
    flexDirection: 'row',
    flexWrap: 'nowrap',
    alignItems: 'flex-start',
    padding: 30
  },
  zipContainer: {
    flex: 1,
    borderBottomColor: '#DDDDDD',
    borderBottomWidth: 1,
    marginLeft: 5,
    marginTop: 3
  },
  zipCode: {
    width: 50,
    height: baseFontSize,
  },
  mainText: {
    flex: 1,
    fontSize: baseFontSize,
    color: '#FFFFFF'
  }
});

module.exports = WeatherProject;
```

Now that we're done, try launching the application. It should work on both Android and iOS, in an emulator or on your physical device. What would you like to change or improve?

You can view the completed application in the GitHub repository (*https://github.com/ bonniee/learning-react-native*).

Summary

For our first real application, we've already covered a lot of ground. We introduced a new UI component, <TextInput>, and learned how to use it to get information from the user. We demonstrated how to implement basic styling in React Native, as well as how to use images and include assets in our application. Finally, we learned how to use the React Native networking API to request data from external web sources. Not bad for a first application!

Hopefully, this has demonstrated how quickly you can build React Native applications with useful features that feel at home on a mobile device.

If you want to extend your application further, here are some things to try:

- Add more images, and change them based on the forecast
- Add validation to the zip code field
- Switch to using a more appropriate keypad for the zip code input
- Display the five-day weather forecast

Once we cover more topics, such as geolocation, you will be able to extend the weather application in even more ways.

Of course, this has been a pretty quick survey. In the next few chapters, we will focus on gaining a deeper understanding of React Native best practices, and look at how to use a lot more features, too!

CHAPTER 4

Components for Mobile

In Chapter 3, we built a simple weather app. In doing so, we touched upon the basics of building interfaces with React Native. In this chapter, we will take a closer look at the mobile-based components used for React Native, and how they compare to basic HTML elements. Mobile interfaces are based on different primitive UI elements than web pages, and thus we need to use different components.

This chapter starts with a more detailed overview of the most basic components: `<View>`, `<Image>`, and `<Text>`. Then, we will discuss how touch and gestures factor into React Native components, and how to handle touch events. Next, we will cover higher-level components, such as the `<ListView>`, `<TabView>`, and `<NavigatorView>`, which allow you to combine other views into standard mobile interface patterns.

Analogies Between HTML Elements and Native Components

When developing for the Web, we make use of a variety of basic HTML elements. These include `<div>`, `<span>`, and `<img>`, as well as organizational elements such as `<ol>`, `<ul>`, and `<table>`. (We could include a consideration of elements such as `<audio>`, `<svg>`, `<canvas>`, and so on, but we'll ignore them for now.)

When dealing with React Native, we don't use these HTML elements, but we use a variety of components that are nearly analogous to them (Table 4-1).

Table 4-1. Analogous HTML and Native components

HTML	React Native
div	View
img	Image
span, p	Text
ul/ol, li	ListView, child items

Although these elements serve roughly the same purposes, they are not interchangeable. Let's take a look at how these components work on mobile with React Native, and how they differ from their browser-based counterparts.

Can I Share Code Between React Native and My Web App?

Unfortunately, React Native's basic components currently can't render to basic HTML elements. Your React Native code can be reused across iOS and Android (and any future React Native platforms), but it can't render to web-compatible views. However, any JavaScript code, including React components, which don't render any basic elements *can* be shared. So, if your business logic is isolated from your rendering code, you can see some reuse there.

The Text Component

Rendering text is a deceptively basic function; nearly any application will need to render text somewhere. However, text within the context of React Native and mobile development works differently from text rendering for the Web.

When working with text in HTML, you can include raw text strings in a variety of elements. Furthermore, you can style them with child tags such as `<strong>` and `<em>`. So, you might end up with an HTML snippet that looks like this:

```
<p>The quick <em>brown</em> fox jumped over the lazy <strong>dog</strong>.</p>
```

In React Native, only `<Text>` components may have plain text nodes as children. In other words, this is not valid:

```
<View>
  Text doesn't go here!
</View>
```

Instead, wrap your text in a <Text> component:

```
<View>
  <Text>This is OK!</Text>
</View>
```

When dealing with <Text> components in React Native, you no longer have access to subtags such as <strong> and <em>, though you can apply styles to achieve similar effects through use of attributes such as fontWeight and fontStyle. Here's how you might achieve a similar effect by making use of inline styles:

```
<Text>
  The quick <Text style={{fontStyle: "italic"}}>brown</Text> fox
  jumped over the lazy <Text style={{fontWeight: "bold"}}>dog</Text>.
</Text>
```

This approach could quickly become verbose. You'll likely want to create styled components as a sort of shorthand when dealing with text, as shown in Example 4-1.

Example 4-1. Creating reusable components for styling text

```
var styles = StyleSheet.create({
  bold: {
      fontWeight: "bold"
  },
  italic: {
      fontStyle: "italic"
  }
});

var Strong = React.createClass({
  render: function() {
    return (
    <Text style={styles.bold}>
      {this.props.children}
    </Text>);
  }
});

var Em = React.createClass({
  render: function() {
    return (
    <Text style={styles.italic}>
      {this.props.children}
    </Text>);
  }
});
```

Once you have declared these styled components, you can freely make use of styled nesting. Now the React Native version looks quite similar to the HTML version (see Example 4-2).

Example 4-2. Using styled components for rendering text

```
<Text>
  The quick <Em>brown</Em> fox jumped
  over the lazy <Strong>dog</Strong>.
</Text>
```

Similarly, React Native does not inherently have any concept of header elements (h1, h2, etc.), but it's easy to declare your own styled <Text> elements and use them as needed.

In general, when dealing with styled text, React Native forces you to change your approach. Style inheritance is limited, so you lose the ability to have default font settings for all text nodes in the tree. One again, Facebook recommends solving this by using styled components:

> You also lose the ability to set up a default font for an entire subtree. The recommended way to use consistent fonts and sizes across your application is to create a component MyAppText that includes them and use this component across your app. You can also use this component to make more specific components like MyAppHeaderText for other kinds of text.
>
> —React Native Documentation

The Text component documentation (*http://bit.ly/1SVQxU3*) has more details on this.

You've probably noticed a pattern here: React Native is very opinionated in its preference for the reuse of styled components over the reuse of styles. We'll discuss this further in the next chapter.

The Image Component

If text is *the* most basic element in an application, images are a close contender, for both mobile and for the Web. When writing HTML and CSS for the Web, we include images in a variety of ways: sometimes we use the <img> tag, while at other times we apply images via CSS, such as when we use the background-image property. In React Native, we have a similar <Image> component, but it behaves a little differently.

The basic usage of the <Image> component is straightforward; just set the source prop:

```
<Image source={require('image!puppies')} />
```

How does that require call work? Where does this resource live? Here's one part of React Native that you'll have to adjust based on which platform you're targeting. On iOS, this means that you'll need to import it into the assets folder within your Xcode project. By providing the appropriate @2x and @3x resolution files, you will enable Xcode to serve the correct asset file for the correct platform. This is a nice change from web development: the relatively limited possible combinations of screen size and resolution on iOS means that it's easier to create targeted assets.

For React Native on other platforms, we can expect that the `image!` require syntax will point to a similar assets directory.

It's worth mentioning that it is also possible to include web-based image sources instead of bundling your assets with your application. Facebook does this as one of the examples in the `UIExplorer` application:

```
<Image source={{uri: 'https://facebook.github.io/react/img/logo_og.png'}}
    style={{width: 400, height: 400}} />
```

When utilizing network resources, you will need to specify dimensions manually.

Downloading images via the network rather than including them as assets has some advantages. During development, for instance, it may be easier to use this approach while prototyping, rather than carefully importing all of your assets ahead of time. It also reduces the size of your bundled mobile application, so that users needn't download all of your assets. However, it means that instead you'll be relying on the user's data plan whenever they access your application in the future. For most cases, you'll want to avoid using the URI-based method.

If you're wondering about working with the user's own images, we'll cover the camera roll in Chapter 6.

Because React Native emphasizes a component-based approach, images *must* be included as an `<Image>` component instead of being referenced via styles. For instance, in Chapter 3, we wanted to use an image as a background for our weather application. Whereas in plain HTML and CSS you would likely use the `background-image` property to apply a background image, in React Native you instead use the `<Image>` as a container component, like so:

```
<Image source={require('image!puppies')}>
  {/* Your content here... */}
</Image>
```

Styling the images themselves is fairly straightforward. In addition to applying styles, certain `props` control how the image will be rendered. You'll often make use of the `resizeMode` prop, for instance, which can be set to `resize`, `cover`, or `contain`. The `UIExplorer` app demonstrates this well (Figure 4-1).

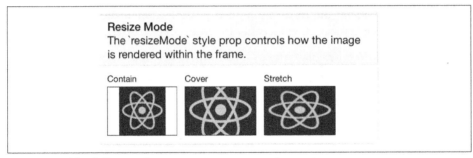

Figure 4-1. The difference between resize, cover, and contain

The `<Image>` component is easy to work with, and very flexible. You will likely make extensive use of it in your own applications.

Working with Touch and Gestures

Web-based interfaces are usually designed for mouse-based controllers. We use things like hover state to indicate interactivity and respond to user interaction. For mobile, it's touch that matters. Mobile platforms have their own norms around interactions that you'll want to design for. This varies somewhat from platform to platform: iOS behaves differently from Android, which behaves differently yet again from Windows Phone.

React Native provides a number of APIs for you to leverage as you build touch-ready interfaces. In this section, we'll look at the `<TouchableHighlight>` container component, as well as the lower-level APIs provided by `PanResponder` and the Gesture Responder system.

Using TouchableHighlight

Any interface elements that respond to user touch (think buttons, control elements, etc.) should usually have a `<TouchableHighlight>` wrapper. `<TouchableHighlight>` causes an overlay to appear when the view is touched, giving the user visual feedback. This is one of the key interactions that causes a mobile application to feel *native*, as opposed to a mobile-optimized website, where touch feedback is limited. As a general rule of thumb, you should use `<TouchableHighlight>` anywhere there would be a button or a link on the Web.

At its most basic usage, you just need to wrap your component in a `<TouchableHighlight>`, which will add a simple overlay when pressed. The `<TouchableHighlight>` component also gives you hooks for events such as `onPressIn`, `onPressOut`, `onLongPress`, and the like, so you can use these events in your React applications.

Example 4-3 shows how you can wrap a component in a `<TouchableHighlight>` in order to give the user feedback.

Example 4-3. Using the `<TouchableHighlight>` component

```
<TouchableHighlight
  onPressIn={this._onPressIn}
  onPressOut={this._onPressOut}
  style={styles.touchable}>
    <View style={styles.button}>
      <Text style={styles.welcome}>
        {this.state.pressing ? 'EEK!' : 'PUSH ME'}
      </Text>
    </View>
</TouchableHighlight>
```

When the user taps the button, an overlay appears, and the text changes (Figure 4-2).

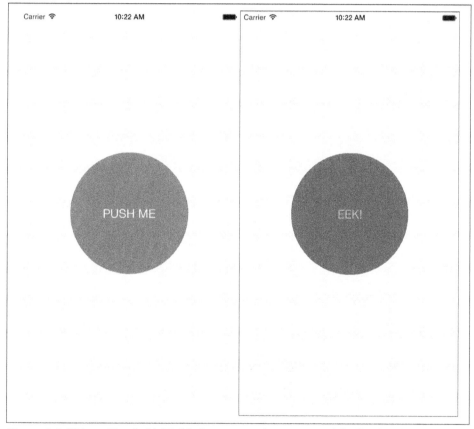

Figure 4-2. Using `<TouchableHighlight>` to give the user visual feedback—the unpressed state (left) and the pressed state, with highlight (right)

This is a contrived example, but it illustrates the basic interactions that make a button "feel" touchable on mobile. The overlay is a key piece of feedback that informs the user that an element can be pressed. Note that in order to apply the overlay, we don't need to apply any logic to our styles; the <TouchableHighlight> handles the logic of that for us.

Example 4-4 shows the full code for this button component.

Example 4-4. Touch/PressDemo.js illustrates the use of <TouchableHighlight>

```
'use strict';

var React = require('react-native');
var {
  StyleSheet,
  Text,
  View,
  TouchableHighlight
} = React;

var Button = React.createClass({
  getInitialState: function() {
    return {
      pressing: false
    }
  },

  _onPressIn: function() {
    this.setState({pressing: true});
  },

  _onPressOut: function() {
    this.setState({pressing: false});
  },

  render: function() {
    return (
      <View style={styles.container}>
        <TouchableHighlight
          onPressIn={this._onPressIn}
          onPressOut={this._onPressOut}
          style={styles.touchable}>

          <View style={styles.button}>
            <Text style={styles.welcome}>
              {this.state.pressing ? 'EEK!' : 'PUSH ME'}
            </Text>
          </View>

        </TouchableHighlight>
      </View>
```

```
    );
  }
});

var styles = StyleSheet.create({
  container: {
    flex: 1,
    justifyContent: 'center',
    alignItems: 'center',
    backgroundColor: '#F5FCFF',
  },
  welcome: {
    fontSize: 20,
    textAlign: 'center',
    margin: 10,
    color: '#FFFFFF'
  },
  touchable: {
    borderRadius: 100
  },
  button: {
    backgroundColor: '#FF0000',
    borderRadius: 100,
    height: 200,
    width: 200,
    justifyContent: 'center'
  },
});

module.exports = Button;
```

Try editing this button to respond to other events, by using hooks like `onPress` and `onLongPress`. The best way to get a sense for how these events map onto user interactions is to experiment using a real device.

The GestureResponder System

What if you want to do more than just make things "tappable"? React Native also exposes two APIs for custom touch handling: `GestureResponder` and `PanResponder`. `GestureResponder` is a lower-level API, while `PanResponder` provides a useful abstraction. We'll start by looking at how the `GestureResponder` system works, because it's the basis for the `PanResponder` API.

Touch on mobile is fairly complicated. Most mobile platforms support multitouch, which means that there can be multiple touch points active on the screen at once. (Not all of these are necessarily fingers, either; think about the difficulty of, for example, detecting the user's palm resting on the corner of the screen.) Additionally, there's the issue of which view should handle a given touch. This problem is similar to how mouse events are processed on the Web, and the default behavior is also similar: the topmost child handles the touch event by default. With React Native's gesture responder system, however, we can override this behavior if we so choose.

The *touch responder* is the view that handles a given touch event. In the previous section, we saw that the `<TouchableHighlight>` component acts as a touch responder. We can cause our own components to become the touch responder, too. The lifecycle by which this process is negotiated is a little complicated. A view that wishes to obtain touch responder status should implement four props:

- `View.props.onStartShouldSetResponder`
- `View.props.onMoveShouldSetResponder`
- `View.props.onResponderGrant`
- `View.props.onResponderReject`

These then get invoked according to the flow illustrated in Figure 4-3, in order to determine if the view will receive responder status.

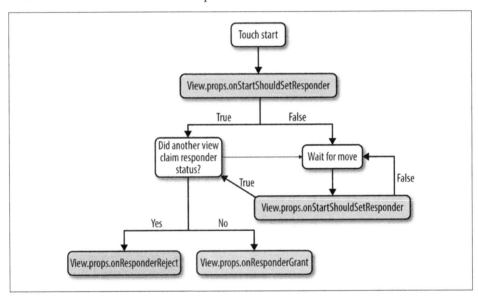

Figure 4-3. Obtaining touch responder status

Yikes, that looks complicated! Let's tease this apart. First, a touch event has three main lifecycle stages: *start*, *move*, and *release* (these correspond to `mouseDown`, `mouseMove`, and `mouseUp` in the browser). A view can request to be the touch responder during the *start* or the *move* phase. This behavior is specified by `onStartShouldSetResponder` and `onMoveShouldSetResponder`. When one of those functions returns `true`, the view attempts to claim responder status.

After a view has attempted to claim responder status, its attempt may be *granted* or *rejected*. The appropriate callback—either `onResponderGrant` or `onResponderReject`—will be invoked.

The responder negotiation functions are called in a bubbling pattern. If multiple views attempt to claim responder status, the deepest component will become the responder. This is typically the desired behavior; otherwise, you would have difficulty adding touchable components such as buttons to a larger view. If you want to override this behavior, parent components can make use of `onStartShouldSetResponderCapture` and `onMoveShouldSetResponderCapture`. Returning `true` from either of these will prevent a component's children from becoming the touch responder.

After a view has successfully claimed touch responder status, its relevant event handlers may be called. Here's the excerpt from the Gesture Responder documentation (*http://bit.ly/1jfZ5ZL*):

`View.props.onResponderMove`
> The user is moving her finger

`View.props.onResponderRelease`
> Fired at the end of the touch (i.e., "touchUp")

`View.props.onResponderTerminationRequest`
> Something else wants to become responder. Should this view release the responder? Returning `true` allows release

`View.props.onResponderTerminate`
> The responder has been taken from the view. It might be taken by other views after a call to `onResponderTerminationRequest`, or by the OS without asking (happens with control center/notification center on iOS)

Most of the time, you will primarily be concerned with `onResponderMove` and `onResponderRelease`.

All of these methods receive a synthetic touch event object, which adheres to the following format (again, excerpted from the documentation):

`changedTouches`
> Array of all touch events that have changed since the last event

`identifier`
> The ID of the touch

`locationX`
> The X position of the touch, relative to the element

locationY
> The Y position of the touch, relative to the element

pageX
> The X position of the touch, relative to the screen

pageY
> The Y position of the touch, relative to the screen

target
> The node id of the element receiving the touch event

timestamp
> A time identifier for the touch, useful for velocity calculation

touches
> Array of all current touches on the screen

You can make use of this information when deciding whether or not to respond to a touch event. Perhaps your view only cares about two-finger touches, for example.

This is a fairly low-level API; if you want to detect and respond to gestures in this way, you will need to spend a decent amount of time tuning the correct parameters and figuring out which values you should care about. In the next section, we will take a look at PanResponder, which supplies a somewhat higher-level interpretation of user gestures.

PanResponder

Unlike <TouchableHighlight>, PanResponder is not a component, but rather a class provided by React Native. It provides a slightly higher-level API than the basic events returned by the Gesture Responder system, while still providing access to those raw events. A PanResponder gestureState object gives you access to the following, in accordance with the PanResponder documentation (*http://bit.ly/1jfZ5ZL*):

stateID
> ID of the gestureState (persisted as long as there at least one touch on screen)

moveX
> The latest screen coordinates of the recently moved touch

moveY
> The latest screen coordinates of the recently moved touch

x0
> The screen coordinates of the responder grant

y0

The screen coordinates of the responder grant

dx

Accumulated distance of the gesture since the touch started

dy

Accumulated distance of the gesture since the touch started

vx

Current velocity of the gesture

vy

Current velocity of the gesture

numberActiveTouches

Number of touches currently on screeen

As you can see, in addition to raw position data, a `gestureState` object also includes information such as the current velocity of the touch and the accumulated distance.

To make use of `PanResponder` in a component, we need to create a `PanResponder` object and then attach it to a component in the `render` method.

Creating a `PanResponder` requires us to specify the proper handlers for `PanResponder` events (Example 4-5).

Example 4-5. Creating a PanResponder requires us to pass a bunch of callbacks

```
this._panResponder = PanResponder.create({
  onStartShouldSetPanResponder: this._handleStartShouldSetPanResponder,
  onMoveShouldSetPanResponder: this._handleMoveShouldSetPanResponder,
  onPanResponderGrant: this._handlePanResponderGrant,
  onPanResponderMove: this._handlePanResponderMove,
  onPanResponderRelease: this._handlePanResponderEnd,
  onPanResponderTerminate: this._handlePanResponderEnd,
});
```

Then, we use spread syntax to attach the `PanResponder` to the view in the component's `render` method (Example 4-6).

Example 4-6. Attaching the PanResponder using spread sytax

```
render: function() {
  return (
    <View
      {...this._panResponder.panHandlers}>
      { /* View contents here */ }
    </View>
```

```
  );
}
```

After this, the handlers that you passed to the `PanResponder.create` call will be invoked during the appropriate move events, if the touch originates within this view.

Example 4-7 shows a modified version of the PanResponder example code provided by React Native. This version listens to touch events on the container view, as opposed to just the circle, and so that the values are printed to the screen as you interact with the application. If you plan on implementing your own gesture recognizers, I suggest experimenting with this application on a real device, so that you can get a feel for how these values respond. Figure 4-4 shows a screenshot of this example, but you'll want to experience it on a device with a real touchscreen.

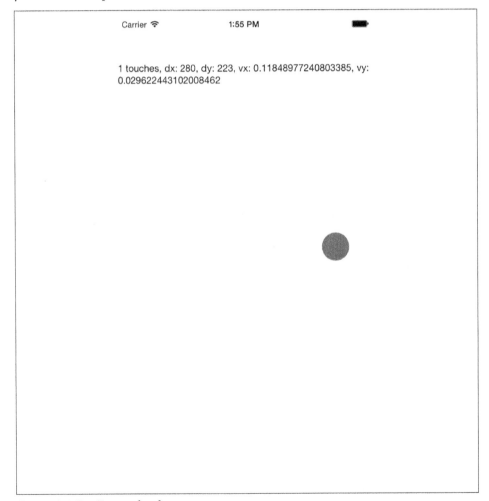

Figure 4-4. PanResponder demo

Example 4-7. Touch/PanDemo.js illustrates the use of PanResponder

```
// Adapted from
// https://github.com/facebook/react-native/blob/master/
// Examples/UIExplorer/PanResponderExample.js

'use strict';

var React = require('react-native');
var {
  StyleSheet,
  PanResponder,
  View,
  Text
} = React;

var CIRCLE_SIZE = 40;
var CIRCLE_COLOR = 'blue';
var CIRCLE_HIGHLIGHT_COLOR = 'green';

var PanResponderExample = React.createClass({

  // Set some initial values.
  _panResponder: {},
  _previousLeft: 0,
  _previousTop: 0,
  _circleStyles: {},
  circle: null,

  getInitialState: function() {
    return {
      numberActiveTouches: 0,
      moveX: 0,
      moveY: 0,
      x0: 0,
      y0: 0,
      dx: 0,
      dy: 0,
      vx: 0,
      vy: 0,
    }
  },

  componentWillMount: function() {
    this._panResponder = PanResponder.create({
      onStartShouldSetPanResponder: this._handleStartShouldSetPanResponder,
      onMoveShouldSetPanResponder: this._handleMoveShouldSetPanResponder,
      onPanResponderGrant: this._handlePanResponderGrant,
      onPanResponderMove: this._handlePanResponderMove,
      onPanResponderRelease: this._handlePanResponderEnd,
      onPanResponderTerminate: this._handlePanResponderEnd,
    });
```

```
    this._previousLeft = 20;
    this._previousTop = 84;
    this._circleStyles = {
      left: this._previousLeft,
      top: this._previousTop,
    };
  },

  componentDidMount: function() {
    this._updatePosition();
  },

  render: function() {
    return (
      <View style={styles.container}>
        <View
          ref={(circle) => {
            this.circle = circle;
          }}
          style={styles.circle}
          {...this._panResponder.panHandlers}/>
        <Text>
          {this.state.numberActiveTouches} touches,
          dx: {this.state.dx},
          dy: {this.state.dy},
          vx: {this.state.vx},
          vy: {this.state.vy}
        </Text>
      </View>
    );
  },

  // _highlight and _unHighlight get called by PanResponder methods,
  // providing visual feedback to the user.
  _highlight: function() {
    this.circle && this.circle.setNativeProps({
      backgroundColor: CIRCLE_HIGHLIGHT_COLOR
    });
  },

  _unHighlight: function() {
    this.circle && this.circle.setNativeProps({
      backgroundColor: CIRCLE_COLOR
    });
  },

  // We're controlling the circle's position directly with setNativeProps.
  _updatePosition: function() {
    this.circle && this.circle.setNativeProps(this._circleStyles);
  },

  _handleStartShouldSetPanResponder:
```

```
    function(e: Object, gestureState: Object): boolean {
      // Should we become active when the user presses down on the circle?
      return true;
    },

    _handleMoveShouldSetPanResponder:
    function(e: Object, gestureState: Object): boolean {
      // Should we become active when the user moves a touch over the circle?
      return true;
    },

    _handlePanResponderGrant: function(e: Object, gestureState: Object) {
      this._highlight();
    },

    _handlePanResponderMove: function(e: Object, gestureState: Object) {
      this.setState({
        stateID: gestureState.stateID,
        moveX: gestureState.moveX,
        moveY: gestureState.moveY,
        x0: gestureState.x0,
        y0: gestureState.y0,
        dx: gestureState.dx,
        dy: gestureState.dy,
        vx: gestureState.vx,
        vy: gestureState.vy,
        numberActiveTouches: gestureState.numberActiveTouches
      });

      // Calculate current position using deltas
      this._circleStyles.left = this._previousLeft + gestureState.dx;
      this._circleStyles.top = this._previousTop + gestureState.dy;
      this._updatePosition();
    },
    _handlePanResponderEnd: function(e: Object, gestureState: Object) {
      this._unHighlight();
      this._previousLeft += gestureState.dx;
      this._previousTop += gestureState.dy;
    },
});

var styles = StyleSheet.create({
  circle: {
    width: CIRCLE_SIZE,
    height: CIRCLE_SIZE,
    borderRadius: CIRCLE_SIZE / 2,
    backgroundColor: CIRCLE_COLOR,
    position: 'absolute',
    left: 0,
    top: 0,
  },
  container: {
```

```
    flex: 1,
    paddingTop: 64,
  },
});

module.exports = PanResponderExample;
```

Choosing how to handle touch

How should you decide when to use the touch and gesture APIs discussed in this section? It depends on what you want to build.

In order to provide the user with basic feedback, and indicate that a button or another element is "tappable," use the `<TouchableHighlight>` component.

In order to implement your own custom touch interfaces, use either the raw Gesture Responder system, or a `PanResponder`. Chances are that you will almost always prefer the `PanResponder` approach, because it also gives you access to the simpler touch events provided by the Gesture Responder system. If you are designing a game, or an application with an unusual interface, you'll need to spend some time building out the interactions you want by using these APIs.

For many applications, you won't need to implement any custom touch handling with either the Gesture Responder system or the `PanResponder`. In the next section, we'll look at some of the higher-level components that implement common UI patterns for you.

Working with Organizational Components

In this section, we're going to look at organizational components that you can use to control general flow within your application. This includes the `<TabView>`, `<NavigatorView>`, and `<ListView>`, which all implement some of the most common mobile interaction and navigational patterns. Once you have planned out your application's navigational flow, you'll find that these components are very helpful in making your application a reality.

Using ListView

Let's start by using the `<ListView>` component. In this section, we are going to build an app that displays the *New York Times* Best Seller List and lets us view data about each book, as shown in Figure 4-5. If you'd like, you can grab your own API token from the *New York Times* (*http://developer.nytimes.com/apps/mykeys*). Otherwise, use the API token included in the sample code.

Figure 4-5. The BookList application we'll be building

Lists are extremely useful for mobile development, and you will notice that many mobile user interfaces feature them as a central element. A `<ListView>` is literally just a list of views, optionally with special views for section dividers, headers, or footers. For example, you can see this interaction pattern in the Dropbox, Twitter, and iOS Settings apps (Figure 4-6).

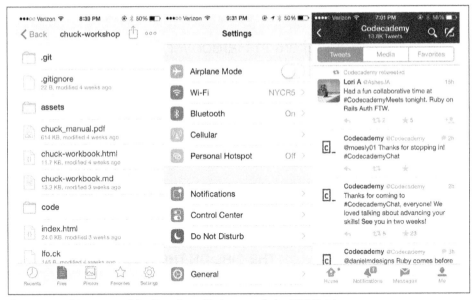

Figure 4-6. Lists as used by Dropbox, Twitter, and the iOS Settings app

<ListView>s are a good example of where React Native shines, because it can leverage its host platform. On mobile, the native <ListView> element is usually highly optimized so that rendering is smooth and stutter-free. If you expect to render a very large number of items in your <ListView>, you should try to keep the child views relatively simple, to try and reduce stutter.

The basic React Native <ListView> component requires two props: dataSource and renderRow. dataSource is, as the name implies, a source of information about the data that needs to be rendered. renderRow should return a component based on the data from one element of the dataSource.

This basic usage is demonstrated in *SimpleList.js*. We'll start by adding a dataSource to our <SimpleList> component. A ListView.DataSource needs to implement the rowHasChanged method. Here's a simple example:

```
var ds = new ListView.DataSource({rowHasChanged: (r1, r2) => r1 !== r2});
```

To set the actual contents of a dataSource, we use cloneWithRows. Let's return the dataSource in our getInitialState call:

```
getInitialState: function() {
  var ds = new ListView.DataSource({rowHasChanged: (r1, r2) => r1 !== r2});
  return {
    dataSource: ds.cloneWithRows(['a', 'b', 'c', 'a longer example', 'd', 'e'])
  };
}
```

The other prop we need is `renderRow`, which should be a function that returns some JSX based on the data for a given row:

```
_renderRow: function(rowData) {
  return <Text style={styles.row}>{rowData}</Text>;
}
```

Now we can put it all together to see a simple `<ListView>`, by rendering a `<ListView>` like so:

```
<ListView
  dataSource={this.state.dataSource}
  renderRow={this._renderRow}
  />
```

It looks like Figure 4-7.

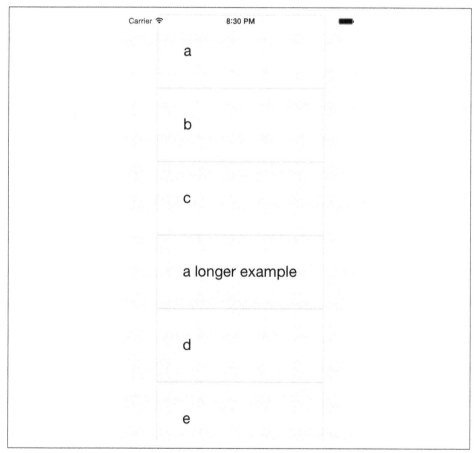

Figure 4-7. The SimpleList component renders a barebones <ListView>

What if we want to do a little more? Let's create a `<ListView>` with more complex data. We will be using the New York Times API to create a simple Best Sellers application, which renders the New York Times Best Seller list.

First, we initialize our data source to be empty, because we'll need to fetch the data:

```
getInitialState: function() {
  var ds = new ListView.DataSource({rowHasChanged: (r1, r2) => r1 !== r2});
  return {
    dataSource: ds.cloneWithRows([])
  };
}
```

Then, we add a method for fetching data, and update the data source once we have it. This method will get called from `componentDidMount`:

```
_refreshData: function() {
  var endpoint =
  'http://api.nytimes.com/svc/books/v3/lists/hardcover-fiction?response-format
  =json&api-key=' + API_KEY;
  fetch(endpoint)
    .then((response) => response.json())
    .then((rjson) => {
      this.setState({
        dataSource: this.state.dataSource.cloneWithRows(rjson.results.books)
      });
    });
}
```

Each book returned by the New York Times API has three properties: `coverURL`, `author`, and `title`. We update the `<ListView>`'s render function to return a component based on those props.

Example 4-8. For _renderRow, we just pass along the relevant data to the <BookItem>

```
_renderRow: function(rowData) {
  return <BookItem coverURL={rowData.book_image}
                   title={rowData.title}
                   author={rowData.author}/>;
},
```

We'll also toss in a header and footer component, to demonstrate how these work (Example 4-9). Note that for a `<ListView>`, the header and footer are not *sticky*; they scroll with the rest of the list. If you want a sticky header or footer, it's probably easiest to render them separately from the `<ListView>` component.

Example 4-9. Adding methods to render header and footer elements in BookListV2.js

```
_renderHeader: function() {
  return (<View style={styles.sectionDivider}>
```

```
      <Text style={styles.headingText}>
        Bestsellers in Hardcover Fiction
      </Text>
      </View>);
  },

  _renderFooter: function() {
    return(
      <View style={styles.sectionDivider}>
        <Text>
          Data from the New York Times Best Seller list.
        </Text>
      </View>
      );
  },
```

All together, the Best Sellers application consists of two files: *BookListV2.js* and *BookItem.js*. *BookListV2.js* is shown in Example 4-10. (*BookList.js* is a simpler file that omits fetching data from an API, and is included in the GitHub repository for your reference.)

Example 4-10. Bestsellers/BookListV2.js

```
'use strict';

var React = require('react-native');
var {
  StyleSheet,
  Text,
  View,
  Image,
  ListView,
} = React;

var BookItem = require('./BookItem');
var API_KEY = '73b19491b83909c7e07016f4bb4644f9:2:60667290';
var QUERY_TYPE = 'hardcover-fiction';
var API_STEM = 'http://api.nytimes.com/svc/books/v3/lists'
var ENDPOINT = `${API_STEM}/${QUERY_TYPE}?response-format=json&api-key=${API_KEY}`;

var BookList = React.createClass({
  getInitialState: function() {
    var ds = new ListView.DataSource({rowHasChanged: (r1, r2) => r1 !== r2});
    return {
      dataSource: ds.cloneWithRows([])
    };
  },

  componentDidMount: function() {
    this._refreshData();
  },
```

```
_renderRow: function(rowData) {
  return <BookItem coverURL={rowData.book_image}
  title={rowData.title}
  author={rowData.author}/>;
},

_renderHeader: function() {
  return (<View style={styles.sectionDivider}>
    <Text style={styles.headingText}>
      Bestsellers in Hardcover Fiction
    </Text>
    </View>);
},

_renderFooter: function() {
  return(
    <View style={styles.sectionDivider}>
      <Text>Data from the New York Times Best Seller list.</Text>
    </View>
    );
},

_refreshData: function() {
  fetch(ENDPOINT)
    .then((response) => response.json())
    .then((rjson) => {
      this.setState({
        dataSource: this.state.dataSource.cloneWithRows(rjson.results.books)
      });
    });
},

render: function() {
  return (
      <ListView
        style=
        dataSource={this.state.dataSource}
        renderRow={this._renderRow}
        renderHeader={this._renderHeader}
        renderFooter={this._renderFooter}
        />
  );
 }
});

var styles = StyleSheet.create({
  container: {
    flex: 1,
    justifyContent: 'center',
    alignItems: 'center',
    backgroundColor: '#FFFFFF',
```

```
    paddingTop: 24
  },
  list: {
    flex: 1,
    flexDirection: 'row'
  },
  listContent: {
    flex: 1,
    flexDirection: 'column'
  },
  row: {
    flex: 1,
    fontSize: 24,
    padding: 42,
    borderWidth: 1,
    borderColor: '#DDDDDD'
  },
  sectionDivider: {
    padding: 8,
    backgroundColor: '#EEEEEE',
    alignItems: 'center'
  },
  headingText: {
    flex: 1,
    fontSize: 24,
    alignSelf: 'center'
  }
});

module.exports = BookList;
```

The <BookItem> is a simple component that handles rendering each child view in the list (Example 4-11).

Example 4-11. Bestsellers/BookItem.js

```
'use strict';

var React = require('react-native');
var {
  StyleSheet,
  Text,
  View,
  Image,
  ListView,
} = React;


var styles = StyleSheet.create({
  bookItem: {
    flex: 1,
```

```
    flexDirection: 'row',
    backgroundColor: '#FFFFFF',
    borderBottomColor: '#AAAAAA',
    borderBottomWidth: 2,
    padding: 5
  },
  cover: {
    flex: 1,
    height: 150,
    resizeMode: 'contain'
  },
  info: {
    flex: 3,
    alignItems: 'flex-end',
    flexDirection: 'column',
    alignSelf: 'center',
    padding: 20
  },
  author: {
    fontSize: 18
  },
  title: {
    fontSize: 18,
    fontWeight: 'bold'
  }
});

var BookItem = React.createClass({
  propTypes: {
    coverURL: React.PropTypes.string.isRequired,
    author: React.PropTypes.string.isRequired,
    title: React.PropTypes.string.isRequired
  },

  render: function() {
    return (
      <View style={styles.bookItem}>
        <Image style={styles.cover} source=/>
        <View style={styles.info}>
          <Text style={styles.author}>{this.props.author}</Text>
          <Text style={styles.title}>{this.props.title}</Text>
        </View>
      </View>
      );
  }
});

module.exports = BookItem;
```

If you have complex data, or very long lists, you will need to pay attention to the performance optimizations enabled by some of <ListView>'s more complex, optional properties. For most uses, however, this will suffice.

Using Navigators

The `<ListView>` is a good example of combining multiple views together into a more usable interaction. On a higher level, we can use components such as the `<Navigator>` to present different screens of an app, much as we might have various pages on a website.

The `<Navigator>` is a subtle but important component, and is used in many common applications. For instance, the iOS Settings app could be implemented as a combination of `<Navigator>` with many `<ListView>` components (Figure 4-8). The Dropbox app also makes use of a Navigator.

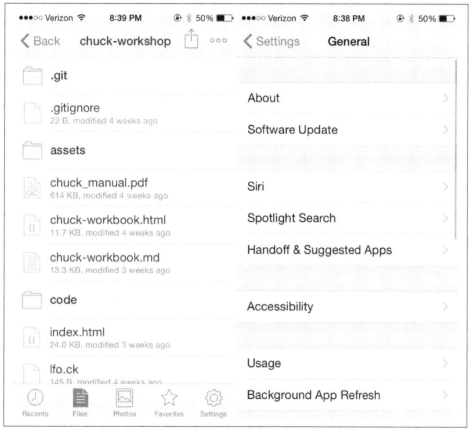

Figure 4-8. The iOS Settings app is a good example of Navigator behavior

A `<Navigator>` allows your application to transition between different screens (often referred to as "scenes"), while maintaining a "stack" of routes, so that you can push, pop, or replace states. You can think of this as analogous to the history API on the Web. A "route" is the title of a screen, coupled with an index.

For instance, in the Settings app, initially the stack is empty. When you select one of the submenus, the initial scene is pushed onto the stack. Tapping "back," in the top-left corner of the screen, will pop it back off.

If you're interested in how this plays out, the UIExplorer app has a good demo of the various ways of using the Navigator API.

Note that there are actually two Navigator options: the cross-platform `<Navigator>` component and the `<NavigatorIOS>` component. In this book, we'll be opting to use the `<Navigator>`.

Should I Use Navigator or NavigatorIOS?

Funny you should ask! The React Native docs have a page addressing that exact question (*http://facebook.github.io/react-native/docs/navigator-comparison.html*). The short answer is: you should use the `<Navigator>`. `<NavigatorIOS>` is not supported by the core team, and hence has some bugs.

The longer answer: `<Navigator>` is a JavaScript reimplementation of the Navigator behavior for both Android and iOS. As such, it's fully cross-platform and flexible. The iOS-specific `<NavigatorIOS>` wraps the UIKit version, so you get Apple's behavior and animations. Its API is more limited, and because it's not a priority for the core team, you probably won't want to use it.

Other Organizational Components

There are plenty of other organizational components, too. For example, a few useful ones include `<TabBarIOS>` and `<SegmentedControlIOS>` (illustrated in Figure 4-9) and `<DrawerLayoutAndroid>` and `<ToolbarAndroid>` (illustrated in Figure 4-10).

You'll notice that these are all named with platform-specific suffixes. That's because they wrap native APIs for platform-specific UI elements.

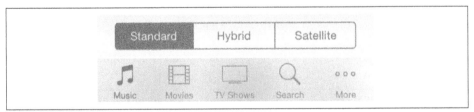

Figure 4-9. An iOS segmented control (top), and an iOS tab bar (bottom)

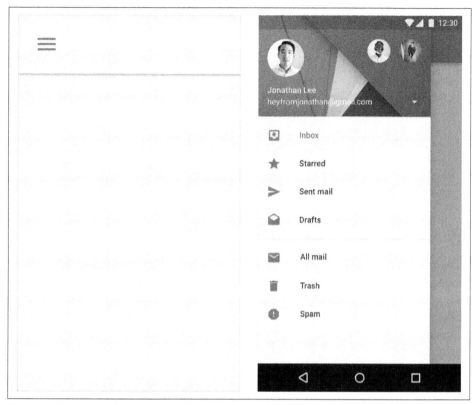

Figure 4-10. An Android toolbar (left), and an Android drawer (right)

These components are very useful for organizing multiple screens within your application. `<TabBarIOS>` and `<DrawerLayoutAndroid>`, for example, give you an easy way to switch between multiple modes or functions. `<SegmentedControlIOS>` and `<Tool barAndroid>` are better suited for more fine-grained controls.

You'll want to refer to the platform-specific design guidelines for how best to use these components:

- Android Design Guide (*http://bit.ly/android_design_guide*)
- iOS Human Interface Guidelines (*http://bit.ly/designing_for_ios*)

But wait! How do we make use of platform-specific components? Let's now take a look at how to handle platform-specific components in cross-platform applications.

Platform-Specific Components

Not all components are available on all platforms, and not all interaction patterns are appropriate for all devices. That doesn't mean that you can't use platform-specific code in your application, though! In this section, we'll cover platform-specific components, as well as strategies for how to incorporate them in your cross-platform applications.

 Writing cross-platform code in React Native is not an all-or-nothing endeavor! You can mix cross-platform and platform-specific code in your application, as we'll do in this section.

iOS- or Android-Only Components

Some components are only available on a specific platform. This includes things like `<TabBarIOS>` or `<SwitchAndroid>`. They're usually platform-specific because they wrap some kind of underlying platform-specific API. For some components, having a platform-agnostic version doesn't make sense. For instance, the `<ToolbarAndroid>` component exposes an Android-specific API for a view type that doesn't exist on iOS anyway.

Platform-specific components are named with an appropriate suffix: either `IOS` or `Android`. If you try to include one on the wrong platform, your application will crash.

Components can also have platform-specific props. These are tagged in the documentation with a small badge indicating their usage. For instance, `<TextInput>` has some props that are platform-agnostic, and others that are specific to iOS or Android (Figure 4-11).

---

ios **maxLength** number

Limits the maximum number of characters that can be entered. Use this instead of implementing the logic in JS to avoid flicker.

android **numberOfLines** number

Sets the number of lines for a TextInput. Use it with multiline set to true to be able to fill the lines.

Figure 4-11. <TextInput> has Android and iOS-specific props

Components with Platform-Specific Versions

So, how do you handle platform-specific components or props in a cross-platform application? The good news is that you can still use these components. Remember how our app has both an *index.ios.js* and an *index.android.js* file? This naming convention can be used for any file, to create a component that has different implementations on Android and iOS.

As an example, we'll use the <SwitchIOS> and <SwitchAndroid> components. They expose slightly different APIs, but what if we just want to use a simple switch? Let's create a wrapper component, <Switch>, which renders the appropriate platform-specific component.

We'll start by implementing *switch.ios.js* (Example 4-12). It's a very simple wrapper around <SwitchIOS>, and allows us to provide a callback for when the switch value changes.

Example 4-12. Switch.ios.js

```
var React = require('react-native');
var { SwitchIOS } = React;

var Switch = React.createClass({
  getInitialState() {
    return {value: false};
  },

  _onValueChange(value) {
    this.setState({value: value});
    if (this.props.onValueChange) {
      this.props.onValueChange(value);
    }
  },

  render() {
    return (
      <SwitchIOS
        onValueChange={this._onValueChange}
        value={this.state.value}/>
    );
  }
});

module.exports = Switch;
```

Next, let's implement *switch.android.js* (Example 4-13).

Example 4-13. Switch.android.js

```
var React = require('react-native');
var { SwitchAndroid } = React;

var Switch = React.createClass({
  getInitialState() {
    return {value: false};
  },

  _onValueChange(value) {
    this.setState({value: value});
    if (this.props.onValueChange) {
      this.props.onValueChange(value);
    }
  },

  render() {
    return (
      <SwitchAndroid
        onValueChange={this._onValueChange}
        value={this.state.value}/>
    );
  }
});
```

```
module.exports = Switch;
```

Note that it looks almost identical to *switch.ios.js*, and it implements the same API. The only difference is that it uses <SwitchAndroid> internally instead of <Switch IOS>.

We can now import our <Switch> component from another file with the syntax:

```
var Switch = require('./switch');
...
var switchComp = <Switch onValueChange={(val) => {console.log(val); }}/>;
```

Let's actually use the <Switch> component. Create a new file, *CrossPlatform.js*, and include the code shown in Example 4-14. We'll have the background color change based on the current value of a <Switch>.

Example 4-14. CrossPlatform.js makes use of the <Switch> component

```
var React = require('react-native');
var {
  StyleSheet,
  Text,
  View,
} = React;
var Switch = require('./switch');
```

```
var CrossPlatform = React.createClass({
  getInitialState() {
    return {val: false};
  },

  _onValueChange(val) {
    this.setState({val: val});
  },

  render: function() {
    var colorClass = this.state.val ? styles.blueContainer : styles.redContainer;
    return (
      <View style={[styles.container, colorClass]}>
        <Text style={styles.welcome}>
          Make me blue!
        </Text>
        <Switch onValueChange={this._onValueChange}/>
      </View>
    );
  }
});

var styles = StyleSheet.create({
  container: {
    flex: 1,
    justifyContent: 'center',
    alignItems: 'center',
  },
  blueContainer: {
    backgroundColor: '#5555FF'
  },
  redContainer: {
    backgroundColor: '#FF5555'
  },
  welcome: {
    fontSize: 20,
    textAlign: 'center',
    margin: 10,
  }
});

module.exports = CrossPlatform;
```

Note that there's no *switch.js* file, but we can call require(*./switch*). The React Native packager will automatically select the correct implementation based on our platform, and use either *switch.ios.js* or *switch.android.js* as appropriate.

Finally, replace the contents of *index.android.js* and *index.ios.js* so that we can render the <CrossPlatform> component.

Example 4-15. The index.ios.js and index.android.js files should be identical, and simply import the crossplatform.js file

```
var React = require('react-native');
var { AppRegistry } = React;
var CrossPlatform = require('./crossplatform');

AppRegistry.registerComponent('PlatformSpecific', () => CrossPlatform);
```

Now we can run our application on both iOS and Android (Figure 4-12).

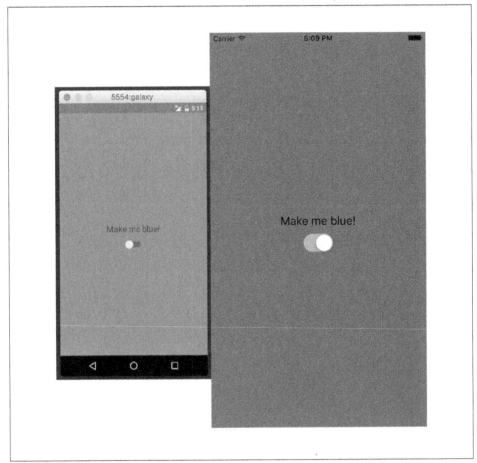

Figure 4-12. The CrossPlatform application should render on both iOS and Android, using the appropriate <Switch> component

When to Use Platform-Specific Components

When is it appropriate to use a platform-specific component? In most cases, you'll want to do so when there's a platform-specific interaction pattern that you want your application to adhere to. If you want your application to feel truly "native," it's worth paying attention to platform-specific UI norms.

Apple and Google both provide human interface guidelines for their platforms, which are worth consulting:

- iOS Human Interface Guidelines (*http://bit.ly/designing_for_ios*)
- Android Design Reference (*http://bit.ly/android_design_reference*)

By creating platform-specific versions of only certain components, you can strike a balance between code reuse and platform-based customization. In most cases, you should only need separate implementations of a handful of components in order to support both iOS and Android.

Summary

In this chapter, we dug into the specifics of a variety of the most important components in React Native. We discussed how to utilize basic low-level components, like `<Text>` and `<Image>`, as well as higher-order components like `<ListView>`, `<Navigator>`, and `<TabBarIOS>`. We also took a look at how to use various touch-focused APIs and components, in case you want to build your own custom touch handlers. Finally, we saw how to use platform-specific components in our applications.

At this point, you should be equipped to build basic, functional applications using React Native! Now that you've acquainted yourself with the components discussed in this chapter, building upon them and combining them to create your own applications should feel remarkably similar to working with React on the Web.

Of course, building up basic, functioning applications is only part of the battle. In the next chapter, we'll focus on styling, and how to use React Native's implementation of styles to get the look and feel you want on mobile.

Styles

It's great to be able to build functional applications, but if you can't style them effectively, you won't get very far! In Chapter 3, we built a simple weather application with some basic styles. While this gave us an overview of how to style React Native components, we glossed over many of the details. In this chapter, we will take a closer look at how styles work in React Native. We'll cover how to create and manage your stylesheets, as well as the details of React Native's implementation of CSS rules. By the end of this chapter, you should feel comfortable creating and styling your own React Native components and applications.

If you want to share styles between your React Native and web applications, the React Style project on GitHub (*https://github.com/js-next/react-style*) provides a version of React Native's style system for the Web.

Declaring and Manipulating Styles

When working with React for the Web, we typically use separate stylesheet files, which may be written in CSS, SASS, or LESS. React Native takes a radically different approach, bringing styles entirely into the world of JavaScript and forcing you to link style objects explicitly to components. Needless to say, this approach tends to provoke strong reactions, as it represents a significant departure from CSS-based styling norms.

To understand the design of React Native's styles, first we need to consider some of the headaches associated with traditional CSS stylesheets.[1] CSS has a number of problems. All CSS rules and class names are global in scope, meaning that styling one

---

1 Christopher Chedeau, aka Vjeux's "CSS in JS" slidedeck (*https://speakerdeck.com/vjeux/react-css-in-js*) provides a good overview.

component can easily break another if you're not careful. For instance, if you include the popular Twitter Bootstrap library, you will introduce over 600 new global variables. Because CSS is not explicitly connected to the HTML elements it styles, dead code elimination is difficult, and it can be nontrivial to determine which styles will apply to a given element.

Languages like SASS and LESS attempt to work around some of CSS's uglier parts, but many of the same fundamental problems remain. With React, we have the opportunity to keep the desirable parts of CSS, but also the freedom for significant divergence. React Native implements a subset of the available CSS styles, focusing on keeping the styling API narrow yet still highly expressive. Positioning is dramatically different, as we'll see later in this chapter. Additionally, React Native does not support pseudoclasses, animations, or selectors. A full list of supported properties can be found in the docs (*https://facebook.github.io/react-native/docs/view.html#style*).

Instead of stylesheets, in React Native we work with JavaScript-based style *objects*. One of React's greatest strengths is that it forces you to keep your JavaScript code— your components—modular. By bringing styles into the realm of JavaScript, React Native pushes us to write modular styles, too.

In this section, we'll cover the mechanics of how these style objects are created and manipulated in React Native.

Inline Styles

Inline styles are the simplest way, syntactically, to style a component in React Native, though they are not usually the *best* way. As you can see in Example 5-1, the syntax for inline styles in React Native is the same as for React for the browser.

Example 5-1. Using inline styles

```
<Text>
  The quick <Text style={{fontStyle: "italic"}}>brown</Text> fox
  jumped over the lazy <Text style={{fontWeight: "bold"}}>dog</Text>.
</Text>
```

Inline styles have some advantages. They're quick and dirty, allowing you to rapidly experiment.

However, you should avoid them in general, because they're less efficient. Inline style objects must be recreated during each render pass. Even when you want to modify styles in response to props or state, you need not use inline styles, as we'll see in a moment.

Styling with Objects

If you take a look at the inline style syntax, you will see that it's simply passing an object to the `style` attribute. There's no need to create the style object in the `render` call, though; instead, you can separate it out, as shown in Example 5-2.

Example 5-2. Style attribute will accept a JavaScript object

```
var italic = {
  fontStyle: 'italic'
};
var bold = {
  fontWeight: 'bold'
};

...

render() {
  return (
    <Text>
      The quick <Text style={italic}>brown</Text> fox
      jumped over the lazy <Text style={bold}>dog</Text>.
    </Text>
    );
}
```

PanDemo.js, from Example 4-7, gives us a good example of a use case in which the immutability provided by `Stylesheet.Create` is a hindrance rather than a help. Recall that we wanted to update the location of a circle based on movement—in other words, each time we received an update from the `PanResponder`, we needed to update state as well as change the styles on the circle. In this circumstance, we don't want immutability at all, at least not for the style controlling the circle's location.

Therefore, we can use a plain object to store the style for the circle.

Using Stylesheet.Create

You will notice that almost all of the React Native example code makes use of `Style Sheet.create`. Using `StyleSheet.create` is strictly optional, but in general you'll want to use it. Here's what the docs (*http://facebook.github.io/react-native/docs/ style.html*) have to say:

> StyleSheet.create construct is optional but provides some key advantages. It ensures that the values are immutable and opaque by transforming them into plain numbers that reference an internal table. By putting it at the end of the file, you also ensure that they are only created once for the application and not on every render.

In other words, `StyleSheet.create` is really just a bit of syntactic sugar designed to protect you. Use it! The vast majority of the time, the immutability provided by `Style Sheet.create` is helpful. It also gives you the ability to do prop validation via prop-Types: styles created with `StyleSheet.create` can be verified using the `View.propTypes.Style` and `Text.propTypes.Style` types.

Style Concatenation

What happens if you want to combine two or more styles?

Recall that earlier we said that we should prefer reusing styled components over styles. That's true, but sometimes style reuse is also useful. For instance, if you have a button style and an `accentText` style, you may want to combine them to create an `AccentButton` component.

If the styles look like this:

```
var styles = Stylesheet.create({
  button: {
    borderRadius: '8px',
    backgroundColor: '#99CCFF'
  },
  accentText: {
    fontSize: 18,
    fontWeight: 'bold'
  }
});
```

Then you can create a component that has *both* of those styles applied through simple concatenation (Example 5-3).

Example 5-3. Style attribute also accepts an array of objects

```
var AccentButton = React.createClass({
  render: function() {
    return (
      <Text style={[styles.button, styles.accentText]}>
        {this.props.children}
      </Text>
    );
  }
});
```

As you can see, the `style` attribute can take an array of style objects. You can also add inline styles here, if you want (Example 5-4).

Example 5-4. You can mix style objects and inline styles

```
var AccentButton = React.createClass({
  render: function() {
    return (
      <Text style={[styles.button, styles.accentText, {color: '#FFFFFF'}]}>
        {this.props.children}
      </Text>
    );
  }
});
```

In the case of a conflict, such as when two objects both specify the same property, React Native will resolve the conflict for you. The rightmost elements in the style array take precedence, and falsy values (`false`, `null`, `undefined`) are ignored.

You can leverage this pattern to apply conditional styles. For example, if we had a `<Button>` component and wanted to apply extra style rules if it's being touched, we could use the code shown in Example 5-5.

Example 5-5. Using conditional styles

```
<View style={[styles.button, this.state.touching && styles.highlight]} />
```

This shortcut can help you keep your rendering logic concise.

In general, style concatenation is a useful tool for combining styles. It's interesting to contrast concatenation with web-based stylesheet approaches: @extend in SASS, or nesting and overriding classes in vanilla CSS. Style concatenation is a more limited tool, which is arguably a good thing: it keeps the logic simple and makes it easier to reason about which styles are being applied and how.

Organization and Inheritance

In most of the examples so far, we append our style code to the end of the main Java-Script file with a single call to `Stylesheet.create`. For example code, this works well enough, but it's not something you'll likely want to do in an actual application. How should we actually organize styles? In this section, we will take a look at ways of organizing your styles, and how to share and inherit styles.

Exporting Style Objects

As your styles grow more complex, you will want to keep them separate from your components' JavaScript files. One common approach is to have a separate folder for each component. If you have a component named `<ComponentName>`, you would create a folder named *ComponentName/* and structure it like so:

```
    - ComponentName
      |- index.js
      |- styles.js
```

Within *styles.js*, you create a stylesheet, and export it (Example 5-6).

Example 5-6. Exporting styles from a JavaScript file

```
'use strict';

var React = require('react-native');
var {
  StyleSheet,
} = React;

var styles = Stylesheet.create({
  text: {
    color: '#FF00FF',
    fontSize: 16
  },
  bold: {
    fontWeight: 'bold'
  }
});

module.exports = styles;
```

Within *index.js*, we can import our styles like so:

```
    var styles = require('./styles.js');
```

Then we can use them in our component (Example 5-7).

Example 5-7. Importing styles from an external JavaScript file

```
'use strict';

var React = require('react-native');
var styles = require('./styles.js');
var {
  View,
  Text,
  StyleSheet
} = React;

var ComponentName = React.createClass({
  render: function() {
    return (
      <Text style={[styles.text, styles.bold]}>
        Hello, world
      </Text>
    );
```

```
  }
});
```

Passing Styles as Props

You can also pass styles as properties. The propType `View.propTypes.style` ensures that only valid styles are passed as props.

You can use this pattern to create extensible components, which can be more effectively controlled and styled by their parents. For example, a component might take in an optional style prop (Example 5-8).

Example 5-8. Components can receive style objects via props

```
'use strict';

var React = require('react-native');
var {
  View,
  Text
} = React;

var CustomizableText = React.createClass({
  propTypes: {
    style: Text.propTypes.Style
  },
  getDefaultProps: function() {
    return {
      style: {}
    };
  },
  render: function() {
    return (
      <Text style={[myStyles.text, this.props.style]}>
        Hello, world
      </Text>
    );
  }
});
```

By adding `this.props.style` to the end of the styles array, we ensure that you can override the default props.

Reusing and Sharing Styles

We typically prefer to reuse styled components, rather than reusing styles, but there are clearly some instances in which you will want to share styles between components. In this case, a common pattern is to organize your project roughly like so:

```
- js
  |- components
     |- Button
        |- index.js
        |- styles.js
  |- styles
     |- styles.js
     |- colors.js
     |- fonts.js
```

By having separate directories for components and for styles, you can keep the intended use of each file clear based on context. A component's folder should contain its React class, as well as any component-specific files. Shared styles should be kept out of component folders. Shared styles may include things such as your palette, fonts, standardized margins and padding, and so on.

styles/styles.js requires the other shared styles files, and exposes them; then your components can require *styles.js* and use shared files as needed. Or, you may prefer to have components require specific stylesheets from the *styles/* directory instead.

Because we've now moved our styles into JavaScript, organizing your styles is really a question of general code organization; there's no single correct approach here.

Positioning and Designing Layouts

One of the biggest changes when working with styling in React Native is positioning. CSS supports a proliferation of positioning techniques. Between `float`, absolute positioning, tables, block layout, and more, it's easy to get lost! React Native's approach to positioning is more focused, relying primarily on flexbox as well as absolute positioning, along with the familiar properties of `margin` and `padding`. In this section, we'll look at how layouts are constructed in React Native, and finish off by building a layout in the style of a Mondrian painting.

Layouts with Flexbox

Flexbox is a CSS3 layout mode. Unlike existing layout modes such as `block` and `inline`, flexbox gives us a direction-agnostic way of constructing layouts. (That's right: finally, vertically centering is easy!) React Native leans heavily on flexbox. If you want to read more about the general specification, the MDN documentation (*http://mzl.la/1Ta8Zcj*) is a good place to start.

With React Native, the following flexbox props are available:

- `flex`
- `flexDirection`
- `flexWrap`

- `alignSelf`
- `alignItems`

Additionally, these related values impact layout:

- `height`
- `width`
- `margin`
- `border`
- `padding`

If you have worked with flexbox on the Web before, there won't be many surprises here. Because flexbox is so important to constructing layouts in React Native, though, we'll spend some time now exploring how it works.

The basic idea behind flexbox is that you should be able to create predictably structured layouts even given dynamically sized elements. Because we're designing for mobile, and need to accommodate multiple screen sizes and orientations, this is a useful feature.

We'll start with a parent `<View>`, and some children:

```
<View style={styles.parent}>
  <Text style={styles.child}> Child One </Text>
  <Text style={styles.child}> Child Two </Text>
  <Text style={styles.child}> Child Three </Text>
</View>
```

To start, we've applied some basic styles to the views, but haven't touched the positioning yet:

```
var styles = StyleSheet.create({
  parent: {
    backgroundColor: '#F5FCFF',
    borderColor: '#0099AA',
    borderWidth: 5,
    marginTop: 30
  },
  child: {
    borderColor: '#AA0099',
    borderWidth: 2,
    textAlign: 'center',
    fontSize: 24,
  }
});
```

The resulting layout is shown in Figure 5-1.

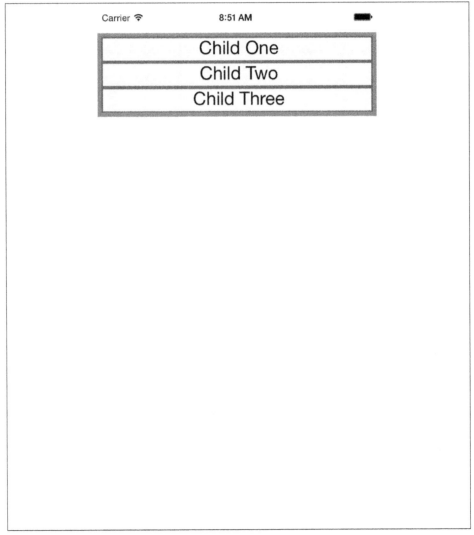

Figure 5-1. The layout before we add flex properties

Next, we will set `flex` on both the parent and the child. By setting the `flex` property, we are explicitly opting in to flexbox behavior. `flex` takes a number. This number determines the relative weight each child gets; by setting it to 1 for each child, we weight them equally.

We also set `flexDirection: 'column'` so that the children are laid out vertically. If we switch this to `flexDirection: 'row'`, the children will be laid out horizontally instead. These changes to the styles can be seen in Example 5-9. Figure 5-2 illustrates the difference in how these values impact the layout.

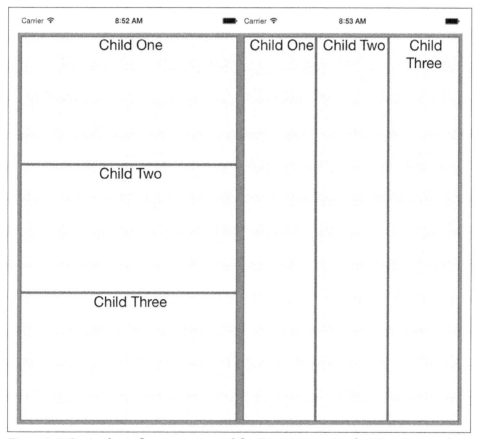

Figure 5-2. Setting basic flex properties and flexDirection; setting flexDirection to column (left) and setting flexDirection to row (right)

Example 5-9. Changing the flex and flexDirection properties

```
var styles = StyleSheet.create({
  parent: {
    flex: 1,
    flexDirection: 'column',
    backgroundColor: '#F5FCFF',
    borderColor: '#0099AA',
    borderWidth: 5,
    marginTop: 30
  },
  child: {
    flex: 1,
    borderColor: '#AA0099',
    borderWidth: 2,
    textAlign: 'center',
    fontSize: 24,
```

```
    }
});
```

If we set `alignItems`, the children will no longer expand to fill all available space in both directions. Because we have set `flexDirection: 'row'`, they will expand to fill the row. However, now they will only take up as much vertical space as they need.

Then, the `alignItems` value determines *where* they are positioned along the cross-axis. The cross-axis is the axis orthogonal to the `flexDirection`. In this case, the cross axis is vertical. `flex-start` places the children at the top, `center` centers them, and `flex-end` places them at the bottom.

Let's see what happens when we set `alignItems` (the result is shown in Figure 5-3):

```
var styles = StyleSheet.create({
  parent: {
    flex: 1,
    flexDirection: 'row',
    alignItems: 'flex-start',
    backgroundColor: '#F5FCFF',
    borderColor: '#0099AA',
    borderWidth: 5,
    marginTop: 30
  },
  child: {
    flex: 1,
    borderColor: '#AA0099',
    borderWidth: 2,
    textAlign: 'center',
    fontSize: 24,
  }
});
```

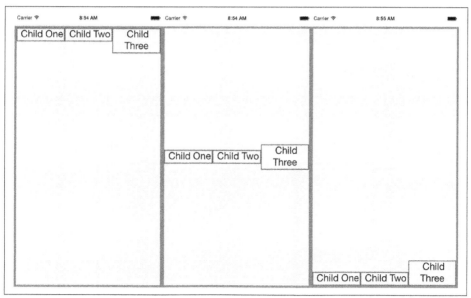

Figure 5-3. Setting alignItems positions children on the cross-axis, which is the axis orthogonal to the flexDirection; here, we see flex-start, center, and flex-end

Using Absolute Positioning

In addition to flexbox, React Native supports absolute positioning. It works much as it does on the Web. You can enable it by setting the position property:

```
position: absolute
```

Then, you can control the component's positioning with the familiar properties of left, right, top, and bottom.

An absolutely positioned child will apply these coordinates relative to its parent's position, so you can lay out a parent element using flexbox and then use absolute position for a child within it.

There are some limitations to this. We don't have z-index, for instance, so layering views on top of each other is a bit complicated. The last view in a stack typically takes precedence.

Absolute positioning can be very useful. For instance, if you want to create a container view that sits below the phone's status bar, absolute positioning makes this easy:

```
container: {
  position: 'absolute',
  top: 30,
  left: 0,
```

```
    right: 0,
    bottom: 0
}
```

Putting It Together

Let's try using these positioning techniques to create a more complicated layout. Say we want to mimic a Mondrian painting. Figure 5-4 shows the end result.

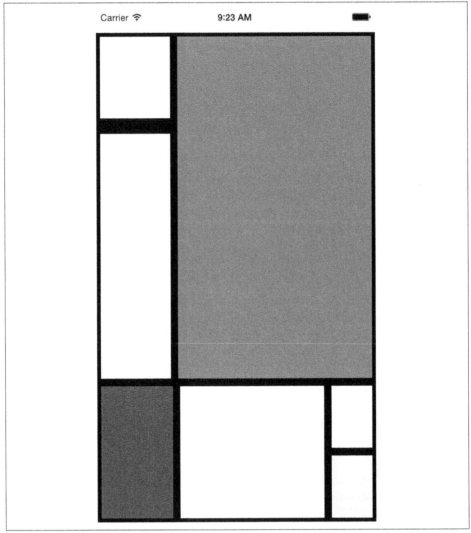

Figure 5-4. We'll use flexbox to construct this layout

How should we go about constructing this kind of layout?

To start with, we create a `parent` style to act as the container. We will use absolute positioning on the parent, because it's most appropriate: we want it to fill all available space, except with a 30-pixel offset at the top, due to the status bar at the top of the screen. We'll also set its `flexDirection` to `column`:

```
parent: {
  flexDirection: 'column',
  position: 'absolute',
  top: 30,
  left: 0,
  right: 0,
  bottom: 0
}
```

Looking back at the image, we can divide the layout up into larger blocks. These divisions are in many ways arbitrary, so we'll pick an option and roll with it. Figure 5-5 shows one way we can segment the layout.

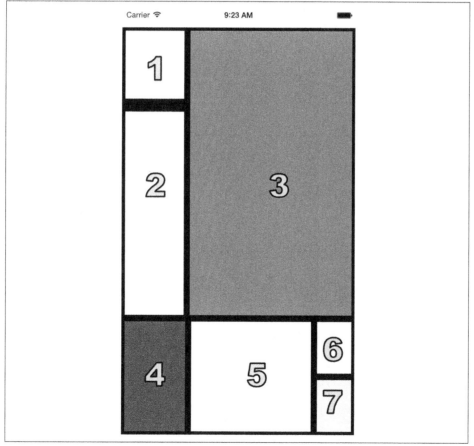

Figure 5-5. The order in which we'll style the sections

We start by cutting the layout into a top and bottom block:

```
<View style={styles.parent}>
  <View style={styles.topBlock}>
  </View>
  <View style={styles.bottomBlock}>
  </View>
</View>
```

Then we add in the next layer. This includes both a "left column" and "bottom right" sector, as well as the actual <View> components for cells three, four, and five:

```
<View style={styles.parent}>
  <View style={styles.topBlock}>
    <View style={styles.leftCol}>
    </View>
    <View style={[styles.cellThree, styles.base]} />
  </View>
  <View style={styles.bottomBlock}>
    <View style={[styles.cellFour, styles.base]}/>
    <View style={[styles.cellFive, styles.base]}/>
    <View style={styles.bottomRight}>
    </View>
  </View>
</View>
```

The final markup contains all seven cells. Example 5-10 shows the full component.

Example 5-10. Styles/Mondrian/index.js

```
'use strict';

var React = require('react-native');
var {
  AppRegistry,
  StyleSheet,
  Text,
  View,
} = React;
var styles = require('./style');

var Mondrian = React.createClass({
  render: function() {
    return (
      <View style={styles.parent}>
        <View style={styles.topBlock}>
          <View style={styles.leftCol}>
            <View style={[styles.cellOne, styles.base]} />
            <View style={[styles.base, styles.cellTwo]} />
          </View>
          <View style={[styles.cellThree, styles.base]} />
        </View>
```

```
        <View style={styles.bottomBlock}>
          <View style={[styles.cellFour, styles.base]}/>
          <View style={[styles.cellFive, styles.base]}/>
          <View style={styles.bottomRight}>
            <View style={[styles.cellSix, styles.base]} />
            <View style={[styles.cellSeven, styles.base]} />
          </View>
        </View>
      </View>
    );
  }
});

module.exports = Mondrian;
```

Now let's add the styles that make it work (Example 5-11).

Example 5-11. Styles/Mondrian/style.js

```
var React = require('react-native');
var { StyleSheet } = React;

var styles = StyleSheet.create({
  parent: {
    flexDirection: 'column',
    position: 'absolute',
    top: 30,
    left: 0,
    right: 0,
    bottom: 0
  },
  base: {
    borderColor: '#000000',
    borderWidth: 5
  },
  topBlock: {
    flexDirection: 'row',
    flex: 5
  },
  leftCol: {
    flex: 2
  },
  bottomBlock: {
    flex: 2,
    flexDirection: 'row'
  },
  bottomRight: {
    flexDirection: 'column',
    flex: 2
  },
  cellOne: {
    flex: 1,
```

```
      borderBottomWidth: 15
    },
    cellTwo: {
      flex: 3
    },
    cellThree: {
      backgroundColor: '#FF0000',
      flex: 5
    },
    cellFour: {
      flex: 3,
      backgroundColor: '#0000FF'
    },
    cellFive: {
      flex: 6
    },
    cellSix: {
      flex: 1
    },
    cellSeven: {
      flex: 1,
      backgroundColor: '#FFFF00'
    }
});

module.exports = styles;
```

Summary

In this chapter, we looked at how styles work in React Native. While in many ways styling is similar to how CSS works on the Web, React Native introduces a different structure and approach to styling. There's plenty of new material to digest here! At this point, you should be able to use styles effectively to create the mobile UIs you need with React Native. And best of all, experimenting with styles is easy: being able to hit "reload" in the simulator grants us a tight feedback loop. (It's worth noting that with traditional mobile development, editing a style would typically require rebuilding your application. Yikes.)

If you want more practice with styles, try going back to the Best Sellers or Weather applications, and adjusting their styling and layouts. As we build more sample applications in future chapters, you'll have plenty of material to practice with, too!

Platform APIs

When building mobile applications, you will naturally want to take advantage of the host platform's specific APIs. React Native makes it easy to access things like the phone's camera roll, location, and persistent storage. These platform APIs are made available to React Native through included modules, which provide us with easy-to-use asynchronous JavaScript interfaces to these functions.

React Native does not wrap *all* of its host platform's functionality by default; some platform APIs will require you to either write your own modules, or use modules written by others in the React Native community. We will cover that process in Chapter 7. The docs (*https://facebook.github.io/react-native/docs/getting-started.html*) are the best place to check if an API is supported.

This chapter covers some of the available platform APIs. For our example, we'll make some modifications to the Weather application from earlier. We'll add geolocation to the app, so that it detects the user's location automatically. We will also add "memory" to the app, so it will remember your previously searched locations. Finally, we'll use the camera roll to change the background image to one of the user's photos.

While relevant code snippets will be presented in each section, the full code for the application is included in "The SmarterWeather Application" on page 119.

iOS and Android Compatibility

Cross-platform support for these APIs is a work in progress, so while `AsyncStorage` is supported on both iOS and Android, geolocation and the camera roll are currently iOS-only. See the list of known issues (*https://facebook.github.io/react-native/docs/known-issues.html*) for which modules are still being ported to Android.

Using Geolocation

For mobile applications, knowing the user's location is often critical. It allows you to serve the user contextually relevant information. Many mobile applications make extensive use of this data.

Happily, React Native has built-in support for geolocation. This is provided as a platform-agnostic "polyfill." It returns data based on the MDN Geolocation API web specification (*http://mzl.la/1lELM6N*). Because we're using the Geolocation specification, you won't need to deal with platform-specific APIs like Location Services, and any location-aware code you write should be fully portable.

> **Geolocation Is Currently iOS-Only**
>
> The Geolocation module will be supported on Android soon, but for now it's iOS-only.

Getting the User's Location

Using the Geolocation API to get a user's location is a breeze. As shown in Example 6-1, we need to make a call to navigator.geolocation.

Example 6-1. Getting the user's location with a navigator.geolocation call

```
navigator.geolocation.getCurrentPosition(
  (position) => {
    console.log(position);
  },
  (error) => {alert(error.message)},
  {enableHighAccuracy: true, timeout: 20000, maximumAge: 1000}
);
```

In conformance to the Geolocation specification, we don't import this API as a separate module; it's simply available for our use.

The getCurrentPosition call takes three arguments: a success callback, an error callback, and a set of geoOptions. Only the success callback is required.

The position object passed to the success callback will contain coordinates, as well as a timestamp. Example 6-2 shows the format and possible values.

Example 6-2. Shape of the response returned from a getCurrentPosition call

```
{
  coords: {
    speed:-1,
```

```
    longitude:-122.03031802,
    latitude:37.33259551999998,
    accuracy:500,
    heading:-1,
    altitude:0,
    altitudeAccuracy:-1
  },
  timestamp:459780747046.605
}
```

geoOptions should be an object, which optionally includes the keys timoeut, enable HighAccuracy, and maximumAge. timeout is probably the most relevant of the bunch when it comes to affecting your application logic.

Handling Permissions

Location data is sensitive information, and therefore will not be accessible to your application by default. Your application should be able to handle permissions being accepted or rejected.

Most mobile platforms have some notion of location permissions. A user may opt to block Location Services entirely on iOS, for instance, or they may manage permissions on a per-app basis. If the user denies your application access, the cancellation callback you pass to getCurrentPosition will be invoked.

It's important to note that location permissions can be revoked at essentially any point in time. Your application should always be prepared for a geolocation call to fail.

The first time your application attempts to access the user's location, the user will be presented with a permissions dialog like the one shown in Figure 6-1.

Figure 6-1. Location request

While this dialog is active, neither callback will fire; once they select an option, the appropriate callback will be invoked. This setting will persist for your application, so the next time, such a check won't be necessary.

If the user denies permissions, you can fail silently if you want, but most apps use an alert dialog to request permissions again.

Testing Geolocation In the iOS Simulator

Chances are you'll be doing most of your testing and development from within a simulator, or at the very least, at your desk. How can you test how your app will behave at different locations?

The iOS simulator allows you to easily spoof a different location. By default, you'll be placed near Apple HQ in California, but you can specify any other coordinates as well by navigating to Debug → Location → Custom Location…, as shown in Figure 6-2.

Figure 6-2. Picking a location

It's good practice to try out different locations as part of your testing process. For rigorous testing, of course, you will want to load your application onto an actual device.

Watching the User's Location

You can also set a watch on the user's location, and receive updates whenever it changes. This can be used to track a user's location over time, or just to ensure that your app receives the most up-to-date position:

```
this.watchID = navigator.geolocation.watchPosition((position) => {
  this.setState({position: position});
});
```

Note that you'll want to clear the watch when your component unmounts as well:

```
componentWillUnmount: function() {
  navigator.geolocation.clearWatch(this.watchID);
}
```

Limitations

Because geolocation is based on the MDN specification, it leaves out more advanced location-based features. For example, iOS provides a Geofencing API, which allows your application to receive notifications when the user enters or leaves a designated geographical region (the geofence). React Native currently does not expose this API.

This means that if you want to use location-based features that aren't currently included in the Geolocation MDN specification, you'll need to port them yourself.

Updating the Weather Application

The SmarterWeather application is an updated version of the Weather application, which now makes use of the Geolocation API. You can see these changes in Figure 6-3.

Most notable is a new component, <LocationButton>, which fetches the user's current location and invokes a callback when pressed. The code for the <LocationButton> is shown in Example 6-3.

Figure 6-3. Displaying forecast based on the user's current location

Example 6-3. SmarterWeather/LocationButton/index.js: when pressed, the button gets the user's location

```
var React = require('react-native');
var styles = require('./style.js');
var Button = require('./../Button');

var LocationButton = React.createClass({
  propTypes: {
    onGetCoords: React.PropTypes.func.isRequired
```

```
    },

    _onPress: function() {
      navigator.geolocation.getCurrentPosition(
        (initialPosition) => {
          this.props.onGetCoords(initialPosition.coords.latitude,
            initialPosition.coords.longitude);
        },
        (error) => {alert(error.message)},
        {enableHighAccuracy: true, timeout: 20000, maximumAge: 1000}
      );
    },

    render: function() {
      return (
        <Button label="Use CurrentLocation"
          style={styles.locationButton}
          onPress={this._onPress}/>
        );
    }
});

module.exports = LocationButton;
```

The Button component used by `LocationButton` is included at the end of this chapter; it simply wraps a `<Text>` component in an appropriate `<TouchableHighlight>` with some basic styling.

We've also had to update the main *weather_project.js* file to accommodate two kinds of queries (Example 6-4). Happily, the OpenWeatherMap API allows us to query by latitude and longitude as well as zip code.

Example 6-4. Adding _getForecastForCoords and _getForecastForZip functions

```
var WEATHER_API_KEY = 'bbeb34ebf60ad50f7893e7440a1e2b0b';
var API_STEM = 'http://api.openweathermap.org/data/2.5/weather?';

...

_getForecastForZip: function(zip) {
  this._getForecast(
    `${API_STEM}q=${zip}&units=imperial&APPID=${WEATHER_API_KEY}`);
},

_getForecastForCoords: function(lat, lon) {
  this._getForecast(
    `${API_STEM}lat=${lat}&lon=${lon}&units=imperial&APPID=${WEATHER_API_KEY}`);
},

_getForecast: function(url, cb) {
  fetch(url)
```

```
    .then((response) => response.json())
    .then((responseJSON) => {
      console.log(responseJSON);
      this.setState({
        forecast: {
          main: responseJSON.weather[0].main,
          description: responseJSON.weather[0].description,
          temp: responseJSON.main.temp
        }
      });
    })
    .catch((error) => {
      console.warn(error);
    });
}
```

Then we include the LocationButton in the main view with _getForecastForCoords as the callback:

```
<LocationButton onGetCoords={this._getForecastForCoords}/>
```

I've omitted the relevant style updates and so on, as the fully updated application code will be included at the end of this chapter.

There's plenty of work left to be done here, if you wanted to actually ship this to users —for example, a more complete app would include better error messages and additional UI feedback. But basic location fetching is surprisingly straightforward!

Accessing the User's Images and Camera

Having access to a phone's local images, as well as the camera, is another critical part of many mobile applications. In this section, we'll explore your options for interacting with users' image data as well as the camera.

We'll still be using the SmarterWeather project. Let's change the background image to use an image from the user's photos.

The CameraRoll Module

React Native provides an interface into the CameraRoll—the images that are stored on the user's phone, taken from the camera.

 CameraRoll Is Currently iOS-Only

The CameraRoll module will be supported on Android soon, but for now it's iOS-only.

Interacting with the CameraRoll, in its most basic form, is not too complicated. First we require the module, as per usual:

```
var React = require('react-native');
var { CameraRoll } = React;
```

Then, we make use of the module to fetch information about the user's photos, as shown in Example 6-5.

Example 6-5. Basic usage of CameraRoll.getPhotos

```
CameraRoll.getPhotos(
  {first: 1},
  (data) => {
    console.log(data);
  },
  (error) => {
    console.warn(error);
  });
```

We make a call to getPhotos with the appropriate query, and it returns some data related to the CameraRoll images.

In SmarterWeather, let's replace the top-level <Image> component with a new component, PhotoBackdrop (Example 6-6). For now, PhotoBackdrop simply pulls the most recent photo from the user's CameraRoll.

Example 6-6. SmarterWeather/PhotoBackdrop/camera_roll_example.js

```
var React = require('react-native');
var { Image, CameraRoll } = React;
var styles = require('./style.js');

var PhotoBackdrop = React.createClass({
  getInitialState() {
    return {
      photoSource: null
    }
  },
  componentDidMount() {
    CameraRoll.getPhotos(
      {first: 5},
      (data) => {
        this.setState({
          photoSource: {uri: data.edges[3].node.image.uri}
        })},
      (error) => {
        console.warn(error);
      });
  },
```

```
  render() {
    return (
      <Image
        style={styles.backdrop}
        source={ this.state.photoSource }
        resizeMode='cover'>
        {this.props.children}
      </Image>
      );
  }
});

module.exports = PhotoBackdrop;
```

`CameraRoll.getPhotos` takes three arguments: an object with params, a success call-back, and an error callback.

Requesting Images with GetPhotoParams

The `getPhotoParams` object can take a variety of options, which are oddly not included in the web documentation. We can take a look at the React Native source code (*http://bit.ly/1kPZnrQ*) to see which options are available to us:

`first`
> number, the number of photos wanted in reverse order of the photo application (i.e., most recent first for `SavedPhotos`)

`after`
> string, a cursor that matches `page_info {end_cursor}` returned from a previous call to `getPhotos`

`groupTypes`
> string, specifies which group to use to filter results. May be *Album*, *All*, *Event*, etc.; full list of `GroupTypes` are specified in the source

`groupName`
> string, specifies a filter on group names, such as *Recent Photos* or an album title

`assetType`
> one of *All*, *Photos*, or *Videos*, specifies a filter on asset type

`mimeTypes`
> array of strings, filters based on mimetype (such as *image/jpeg*)

In our basic invocation of `getPhotos` in Example 6-5, our `getPhotoParams` object was quite simple:

```
{first: 1}
```

This means, simply, that we were looking for the most recent photo.

Rendering an Image from the Camera Roll

How do we render an image we've received from the camera roll? Let's take a look at that success callback:

```
(data) => {
  this.setState({
    photoSource: {uri: data.edges[0].node.image.uri}
  })},
```

The structure of the data object is not immediately apparent, so you'll likely want to use the debugger to inspect the object. Each of the objects in data.edges has a node that represents a photo; from there, you can get the URI of the actual asset.

You may recall that an <Image> component can take a URI as its source property. So, we can render an image obtained from the camera roll by setting the source property appropriately:

```
<Image source={this.state.photoSource} />
```

That's it! You can see the resulting application, including the image, in Figure 6-4.

Figure 6-4. Rendering an image from the CameraRoll

Displaying a List of Photos

In many apps, we give the user the ability to select a photo. How do you render that photo selection screen?

If you're an iOS user, you may have noticed that while there is a default iOS photo selection screen, many applications actually implement their own custom screen. As shown in Figure 6-5, Twitter and Tumblr both have custom screens. In Twitter's case, this allows you to select a photo from the Tweet composition screen.

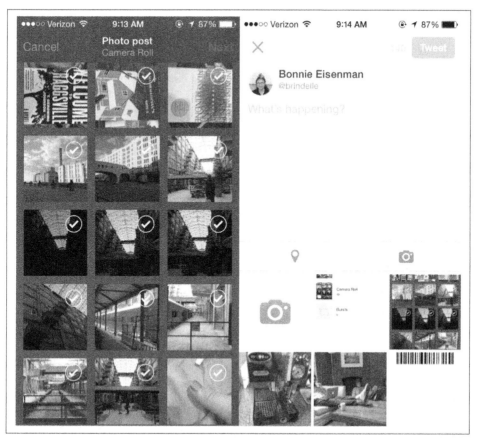

Figure 6-5. Photo selection screens in the Tumblr (left) and Twitter (right) iOS applications

The default screen is a full-page dialog, and it looks a bit different (Figure 6-6).

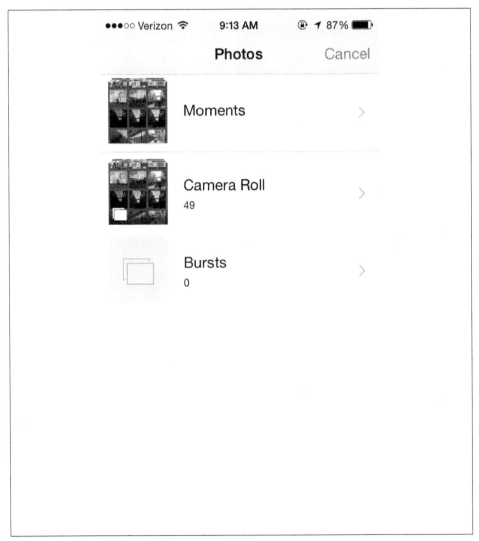

Figure 6-6. Default dialog

So, you can either use the built-in element for this, or roll your own. Applications often build custom solutions in order to provide additional functionality over the standard interface. The UIExplorer application (*https://github.com/facebook/react-native/tree/master/Examples/UIExplorer*) gives us a very basic example of how to use the CameraRoll to create a simple custom view of the user's photo library, shown in Figure 6-7.

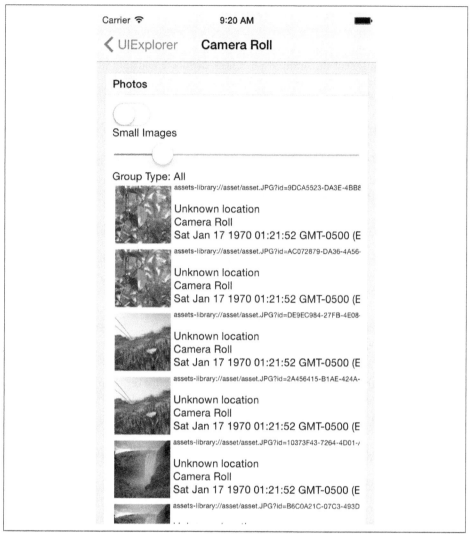

Figure 6-7. The CameraRoll example from the UIExplorer application

It's little more than the `CameraRoll` interactions we saw earlier, couped with a `<List View>`. You could use this approach to develop a cross-platform image selection component for both Android and iOS.

On iOS, the native UI element is the `UIImagePickerController`, which React Native supports via the `ImagePickerIOS` module.

Android Support for Photo Selection

Currently, React Native provides the `ImagePickerIOS` API for selecting photos or accessing the camera on iOS, but there isn't an equivalent for Android yet. Check the documentation (*https://face book.github.io/react-native/docs*) for the most up-to-date information.

You can import the `ImagePickerIOS` module in the usual way:

```
var { ImagePickerIOS } = React;
```

Then, using it is simple. We can query `ImagePickerIOS` to see if we are able to use the camera or record videos (Example 6-7).

Example 6-7. Checking if we may access the camera or record videos using ImagePickerIOS

```
ImagePickerIOS.canUseCamera((result) => {
  console.log(result); // boolean
});

ImagePickerIOS.canRecordVideos((result) => {
  console.log(result); // boolean
});
```

Then, to trigger the photo selection dialog, we call `openSelectDialog`, furnishing it with some options as well as callbacks for successful photo selection, and user cancellation (Example 6-8).

Example 6-8. Triggering the photo selection dialog using ImagePickerIOS

```
ImagePickerIOS.openSelectDialog(
  {
    showImages: true,
    showVideos: false,
  },
  (data) => {
    this.setState({
      photoSource: {uri: data}
    });
  },
  () => {
    console.log('User canceled the action');
  });
```

This call opens up the standard iOS photo selection dialog (Figure 6-8).

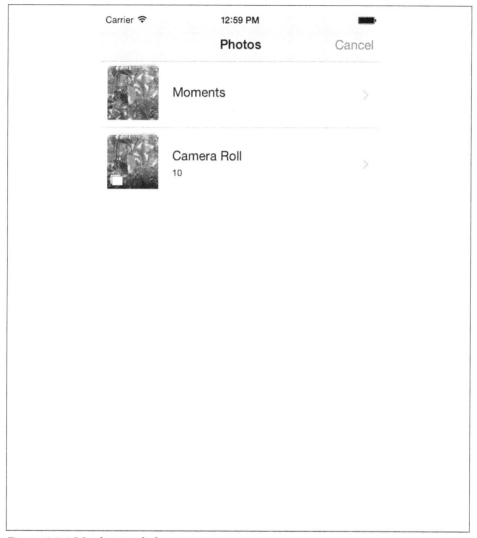

Figure 6-8. iOS selection dialog

The data passed to the success callback is a URI, which can be used as an `<Image>` source prop.

Uploading an Image to a Server

What if you want to upload a photo somewhere? React Native ships with built-in image uploading functionality in the XHR module. The UIExplorer example demonstrates (*http://bit.ly/1jjz37G*) one approach:

```
var formdata = new FormData();
...
formdata.append('image', {...this.state.randomPhoto, name: 'image.jpg'});
...
xhr.send(formdata);
```

XHR is short for `XMLHttpRequest`. React Native implements the XHR API on top of the iOS networking APIs. Similar to geolocation, React Native's XHR implementation is based on the MDN specification (*http://bit.ly/xmlhttpreq*).

Using XHR for network requests is somewhat more complex, compared with the Fetch API, but the basic approach should look something like Example 6-9.

Example 6-9. Basic structure for POSTing a photo using XHR

```
var xhr = new XMLHttpRequest();
xhr.open('POST', 'http://posttestserver.com/post.php');
var formdata = new FormData();
formdata.append('image', {...this.state.photo, name: 'image.jpg'});
xhr.send(formdata);
```

Omitted here are the various callbacks you will want to register with the XHR request.

Storing Persistent Data with AsyncStore

Most applications will need to keep track of some variety of data, persistently. How do you accomplish this with React Native?

iOS provides us with `AsyncStorage`, a key-value store that is global to your application. If you have used `LocalStorage` on the Web, `AsyncStorage` ought to feel quite similar. `AsyncStorage`, as the name suggests, is asynchronous; its API is quite simple, too, and a React Native module for it is included by default. Let's take a look at how to use it.

The storage key used by `AsyncStorage` can be any string; it's customary to use the format `@AppName:key`, like so:

```
var STORAGE_KEY = '@SmarterWeather:zip';
```

The `AsyncStorage` module returns a promise in response to both `getItem` and `setItem`. For `SmarterWeather`, let's load the stored zip code in `componentDidMount`:

```
AsyncStorage.getItem(STORAGE_KEY)
  .then((value) => {
    if (value !== null) {
      this._getForecastForZip(value);
    }
  })
```

```
    .catch((error) => console.log('AsyncStorage error: ' + error.message))
    .done();
```

Then, in _getForecaseForZip, we can store the zip code value:

```
AsyncStorage.setItem(STORAGE_KEY, zip)
    .then(() => console.log('Saved selection to disk: ' + zip))
    .catch((error) => console.log('AsyncStorage error: ' + error.message))
    .done();
```

AsyncStorage also provides methods for deleting keys, merging keys, and fetching all available keys.

Other Storage Options

If you are working with more complicated, structured data, or simply *more* of it, you will likely want options beyond a simple key-value store.

One common database on iOS is SQLite; however, this is not available as a built-in React Native module. In the next chapter, we will look at how to wrap native modules for use with React Native, and how to install modules that others have written.

The SmarterWeather Application

All of the example code in this chapter can be found in the *SmarterWeather/* directory. The application from Chapter 3 has changed quite a bit, so let's take a look at the structure of the entire appliation again (Figure 6-9).

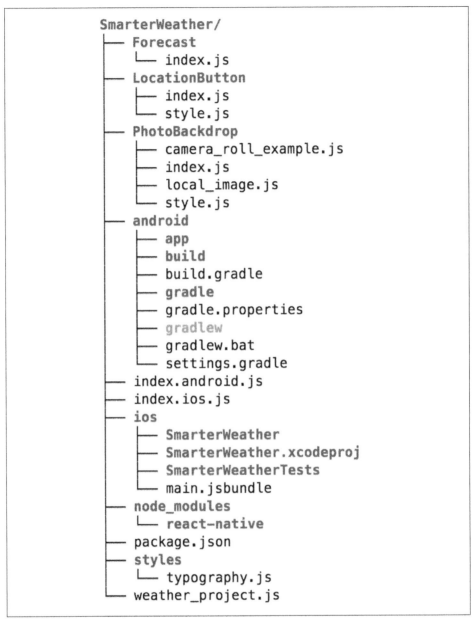

```
SmarterWeather/
├── Forecast
│   └── index.js
├── LocationButton
│   ├── index.js
│   └── style.js
├── PhotoBackdrop
│   ├── camera_roll_example.js
│   ├── index.js
│   ├── local_image.js
│   └── style.js
├── android
│   ├── app
│   ├── build
│   ├── build.gradle
│   ├── gradle
│   ├── gradle.properties
│   ├── gradlew
│   ├── gradlew.bat
│   └── settings.gradle
├── index.android.js
├── index.ios.js
├── ios
│   ├── SmarterWeather
│   ├── SmarterWeather.xcodeproj
│   ├── SmarterWeatherTests
│   └── main.jsbundle
├── node_modules
│   └── react-native
├── package.json
├── styles
│   └── typography.js
└── weather_project.js
```

Figure 6-9. Contents of the SmarterWeather project

The top-level component is located in *weather_project.js*. Shared font styles are located in *styles/typography.js*. The folders *Forecast/*, *PhotoBackdrop/*, *Button/*, and *LocationButton/* all contain React components used in the new SmarterWeather application.

The WeatherProject Component

The top-level component is located in *weather_project.js* (Example 6-10). This includes the use of `AsyncStorage` to store the most recent location.

Example 6-10. SmarterWeather/weather_project.js

```
var React = require('react-native');
var {
  StyleSheet,
  Text,
  View,
  TextInput,
  AsyncStorage,
  Image
} = React;

var Forecast = require('./Forecast');
var LocationButton = require('./LocationButton');
var STORAGE_KEY = '@SmarterWeather:zip';
var WEATHER_API_KEY = 'bbeb34ebf60ad50f7893e7440a1e2b0b';
var API_STEM = 'http://api.openweathermap.org/data/2.5/weather?';

// This version uses flowers.png from local assets
// var PhotoBackdrop = require('./PhotoBackdrop/local_image');

// This version has you to pick a photo
var PhotoBackdrop = require('./PhotoBackdrop');

// This version pulls a specified photo from the camera roll
// var PhotoBackdrop = require('./PhotoBackdrop/camera_roll_example');

var WeatherProject = React.createClass({
  getInitialState() {
    return {
      forecast: null
    };
  },

  componentDidMount: function() {
    AsyncStorage.getItem(STORAGE_KEY)
      .then((value) => {
        if (value !== null) {
          this._getForecastForZip(value);
        }
      })
      .catch((error) => console.log('AsyncStorage error: ' + error.message))
      .done();
  },

  _getForecastForZip: function(zip) {
```

```
      // Store zip code
      AsyncStorage.setItem(STORAGE_KEY, zip)
        .then(() => console.log('Saved selection to disk: ' + zip))
        .catch((error) => console.log('AsyncStorage error: ' + error.message))
        .done();

      this._getForecast(
        `${API_STEM}q=${zip}&units=imperial&APPID=${WEATHER_API_KEY}`);
    },

    _getForecastForCoords: function(lat, lon) {
      this._getForecast(
        `${API_STEM}lat=${lat}&lon=${lon}&units=imperial&APPID=${WEATHER_API_KEY}`);
    },

    _getForecast: function(url, cb) {
      fetch(url)
        .then((response) => response.json())
        .then((responseJSON) => {
          console.log(responseJSON);
          this.setState({
            forecast: {
              main: responseJSON.weather[0].main,
              description: responseJSON.weather[0].description,
              temp: responseJSON.main.temp
            }
          });
        })
        .catch((error) => {
          console.warn(error);
        });
    },

    _handleTextChange: function(event) {
      var zip = event.nativeEvent.text;
      this._getForecastForZip(zip);
    },

    render: function() {
      var content = null;
      if (this.state.forecast !== null) {
        content = (
          <View style={styles.row}>
            <Forecast
              main={this.state.forecast.main}
              description={this.state.forecast.description}
              temp={this.state.forecast.temp}/>
          </View>);
      }

      return (
        <PhotoBackdrop>
```

```
            <View style={styles.overlay}>
             <View style={styles.row}>
               <Text style={textStyles.mainText}>
                 Current weather for
               </Text>
               <View style={styles.zipContainer}>
                 <TextInput
                   style={[textStyles.mainText, styles.zipCode]}
                   returnKeyType='go'
                   onSubmitEditing={this._handleTextChange}/>
               </View>
             </View>
             <View style={styles.row}>
               <LocationButton onGetCoords={this._getForecastForCoords}/>
             </View>
             {content}
            </View>
          </PhotoBackdrop>
      );
    }
});

var textStyles = require('./styles/typography.js');
var styles = StyleSheet.create({
  overlay: {
    paddingTop: 5,
    backgroundColor: '#000000',
    opacity: 0.5,
  },
  row: {
    width: 400,
    flex: 1,
    flexDirection: 'row',
    flexWrap: 'nowrap',
    alignItems: 'center',
    justifyContent: 'center',
    padding: 30
  },
  zipContainer: {
    flex: 1,
    borderBottomColor: '#DDDDDD',
    borderBottomWidth: 1,
    marginLeft: 5,
    marginTop: 3,
    width: 10
  },
  zipCode: {
    width: 50,
    height: textStyles.baseFontSize,
  }
});
```

```
module.exports = WeatherProject;
```

It makes use of shared styles located in *styles/typography.js* (Example 6-11).

Example 6-11. Shared font styles are located in SmarterWeather/styles/typography.js

```
var React = require('react-native');
var { StyleSheet } = React;

var baseFontSize = 18;

var styles = StyleSheet.create({
  bigText: {
    fontSize: baseFontSize + 8,
    color: '#FFFFFF'
  },
  mainText: {
    fontSize: baseFontSize,
    color: '#FFFFFF'
  }
});

// For use elsewhere...
styles['baseFontSize'] = baseFontSize;

module.exports = styles;
```

The Forecast Component

This component displays the forecast information, including the temperature. It's used by the <WeatherProject> component above. The code for the <Forecast> component is provided in Example 6-12.

Example 6-12. Forecast component renders information about the forecast

```
var React = require('react-native');
var { Text, View, StyleSheet } = React;
var styles = require('../styles/typography.js');

var Forecast = React.createClass({
  render: function() {
    return (
      <View style={forecastStyles.forecast}>
        <Text style={styles.bigText}>
          {this.props.main}
        </Text>
        <Text style={styles.mainText}>
          Current conditions: {this.props.description}
        </Text>
      </View>
```

```
      <Text style={styles.bigText}>
        {this.props.temp}°F
      </Text>
    </View>
  );
  }
});

var forecastStyles = StyleSheet.create({
  forecast: {
    alignItems: 'center'
  }
});

module.exports = Forecast;
```

The Button Component

The `<Button>` component is a reusable container-style component. It provides a properly-styled `<Text>` wrapped by a `<TouchableHighlight>`. The main component file is provided in Example 6-13, and its associated styles are provided in Example 6-14.

Example 6-13. Button component provides an appropriately styled
`<TouchableHighlight>` containing a `<Text>`

```
var React = require('react-native');
var {
  Text,
  View,
  TouchableHighlight
} = React;
var styles = require('./style.js');

var Button = React.createClass({
  propTypes: {
    onPress: React.PropTypes.func,
    label: React.PropTypes.string
  },

  render: function() {
    return (
      <TouchableHighlight onPress={this.props.onPress}>
        <View style={[styles.button, this.props.style]}>
          <Text>
            {this.props.label}
          </Text>
        </View>
      </TouchableHighlight>
    );
  }
```

```
});

module.exports = Button;
```

Example 6-14. Styles for the Button component

```
var React = require('react-native');
var { StyleSheet } = React;

var baseFontSize = 16;

var styles = StyleSheet.create({
  button: {
    backgroundColor: '#FFDDFF',
    width: 200,
    padding: 25,
    borderRadius: 5
  },
});

module.exports = styles;
```

The LocationButton Component

When pressed, the <LocationButton> fetches the user's location and invokes a call-back. The component's main JavaScript file is provided in Example 6-15, and its styles are provided in Example 6-16.

Example 6-15. <LocationButton> component

```
var React = require('react-native');
var styles = require('./style.js');
var Button = require('./../Button');

var LocationButton = React.createClass({
  propTypes: {
    onGetCoords: React.PropTypes.func.isRequired
  },

  _onPress: function() {
    navigator.geolocation.getCurrentPosition(
      (initialPosition) => {
        this.props.onGetCoords(initialPosition.coords.latitude,
          initialPosition.coords.longitude);
      },
      (error) => {alert(error.message)},
      {enableHighAccuracy: true, timeout: 20000, maximumAge: 1000}
    );
  },
```

```
render: function() {
  return (
    <Button label="Use CurrentLocation"
      style={styles.locationButton}
      onPress={this._onPress}/>
    );
  }
});

module.exports = LocationButton;
```

Example 6-16. Styles for <LocationButton>

```
var React = require('react-native');
var { StyleSheet } = React;

var baseFontSize = 16;

var styles = StyleSheet.create({
  locationButton: {
    backgroundColor: '#FFDDFF',
    width: 200,
    padding: 25,
    borderRadius: 5
  },
});

module.exports = styles;
```

The PhotoBackdrop Component

There are three versions of <PhotoBackdrop> provided, to demonstrate different methods of selecting an image for the background. The first, provided in Example 6-17 and listed as *local_image.js* in the Github repository, uses a simple require call to load a standard image asset. The second, as seen in Example 6-18 and provided as *camera_roll_example.js* in the Github repository, selects an image from the user's CameraRoll. Finally, the third version, is provided in Example 6-19 and as *index.js* in the Github repository. This version uses ImagePickerIOS to prompt the user to select a background image.

Example 6-17. local_image.js is the original version; it uses a simple require call

```
var React = require('react-native');
var { Image } = React;
var styles = require('./style.js');

var PhotoBackdrop = React.createClass({
  render() {
    return (
```

```
        <Image
          style={styles.backdrop}
          source={require('image!flowers')}
          resizeMode='cover'>
          {this.props.children}
        </Image>
      );
  }
});

module.exports = PhotoBackdrop;
```

*Example 6-18. camera_roll_example.js programmatically selects an image from the
CameraRoll*

```
var React = require('react-native');
var { Image, CameraRoll } = React;
var styles = require('./style.js');

var PhotoBackdrop = React.createClass({
  getInitialState() {
    return {
      photoSource: null
    }
  },
  componentDidMount() {
    CameraRoll.getPhotos(
      {first: 5},
      (data) => {
        this.setState({
          photoSource: {uri: data.edges[3].node.image.uri}
        })},
      (error) => {
        console.warn(error);
      });
  },
  render() {
    return (
      <Image
        style={styles.backdrop}
        source={ this.state.photoSource }
        resizeMode='cover'>
        {this.props.children}
      </Image>
      );
  }
});

module.exports = PhotoBackdrop;
```

Example 6-19. index.js, the final version, uses ImagePickerIOS and asks the user to select an image

```
var React = require('react-native');
var {
  Image,
  ImagePickerIOS
} = React;
var styles = require('./style.js');

var Button = require('./../Button');

var PhotoBackdrop = React.createClass({
  getInitialState() {
    return {
      photoSource: require('image!flowers')
    }
  },
  _pickImage() {
    ImagePickerIOS.openCameraDialog(
      {},
      (data) => {
        this.setState({
          photoSource: {uri: data}
        });
      },
      () => {
        console.log('User canceled the action');
      });
  },
  render() {
    return (
      <Image
        style={styles.backdrop}
        source={ this.state.photoSource }
        resizeMode='cover'>
        {this.props.children}
        <Button
          style={styles.button}
          label="Load Image"
          onPress={this._pickImage}/>
      </Image>
      );
  }
});

module.exports = PhotoBackdrop;
```

All three versions share the same stylesheet, shown below in Example 6-20.

Example 6-20. All three versions of the <PhotoBackdrop> use this stylesheet

```
var React = require('react-native');
var { StyleSheet } = React;

var styles = StyleSheet.create({
  backdrop: {
    flex: 1,
    flexDirection: 'column'
  },
  button: {
    flex: 1,
    margin: 100,
    alignItems: 'center'
  }
});

module.exports = styles;
```

Summary

In this chapter, we made some modifications to the Weather application. We looked at the Geolocation, Camera Roll, and AsyncStorage APIs, and learned how to incorporate these modules into our applications. Because support for these APIs varies by platform, you'll want to isolate components that make use of them, so that you can provide platform-agnostic wrappers around them, like we saw in Chapter 4.

Issues of compatibility aside, when React Native ships with support for a host platform API, it makes usage a breeze. But what happens if React Native does not yet support a given API, such as in the case of video playback, and you want to use a library or module that isn't yet available in JavaScript? In the next chapter, we'll take a closer look at this scenario.

Modules

In Chapter 6, we looked at some of the APIs that React Native exposes for interacting with the host platform. Things like the camera roll and geolocation are platform-specific, but React Native exposes interfaces for them for our convenience. Because support for those APIs is built into React Native, they're quite easy to use.

What happens when we want to use an API that isn't supported by React Native? In this chapter, we'll look at how to install modules written by members of the React Native community using npm. We'll also take a closer look at one such module for iOS, react-native-video, and learn how the RCTBridgeModule can allow you to add JavaScript interfaces to existing Objective-C APIs. We'll also look at importing pure JavaScript libraries into your project, and how to manage dependencies.

While we'll be looking at some Objective-C and Java code this chapter, don't be alarmed! We'll be taking it slowly. A full introduction to mobile development for iOS and Android is beyond the scope of this book, but we'll walk through some examples together.

Installing JavaScript Libraries with npm

Before we discuss how native modules work, first we should cover how to install external dependenies in general. React Native uses npm to manage dependencies. npm is the package manager for Node.js, but the npm registry includes packages for all sorts of JavaScript projects, not just Node. npm uses a file called *package.json* to store metadata about your project, including the list of dependencies.

Let's start by creating a fresh project:

```
react-native init Depends
```

After creating a new project, your *package.json* will look something like this:

```
{
  "name": "Depends",
  "version": "0.0.1",
  "private": true,
  "scripts": {
    "start": "node_modules/react-native/packager/packager.sh"
  },
  "dependencies": {
    "react-native": "^0.12.0"
  }
}
```

Note that for now, the only top-level dependency in your project is react-native. Let's add another dependency!

The lodash library is similar to Underscore.js; it provides a number of helpful utility functions, like a shuffle function for arrays. We install it with the --save flag to indicate that it should be added to our list of dependencies:

```
npm install --save lodash
```

Now your dependencies hash in *package.json* should be updated:

```
"dependencies": {
  "lodash": "^3.10.1",
  "react-native": "^0.12.0"
}
```

If you want to use lodash in your React Native application, you can now require it by name:

```
var _ = require('lodash');
```

Let's use lodash to print a random number:

```
var _ = require('lodash');
console.log('Random number: ' + _.random(0, 5));
```

It works! But what about other modules? Can you include arbitrary packages by using npm install?

The answer is "yes," with some caveats. Any methods that touch the DOM, for instance, will fail. Integrating with existing packages may require some finagling, because so many packages make assumptions about the environment they'll be running in. But in general, you can take advantage of arbitrary JavaScript packages, and use npm to manage your dependencies just like you would on any other JavaScript project.

Native Modules for iOS

Now that we've seen what it's like to add an outside JavaScript library, let's add a React Native component using npm. For this section, we are going to be using `react-native-video`, a React Native component implemented by Brent Vatne, as our primary example. This module provides us with a `<Video>` component, which can be used (surprise!) to play videos. Then, we'll peek under the hood and see how native modules work with Objective-C and iOS.

Including a Third-Party Component

The `react-native-video` component is listed in the npm registry (*https://www.npmjs.com/package/react-native-video*). We can add it to our project with `npm install`:

```
npm install react-native-video --save
```

If we were working with traditional web development, we would be done! `react-native-video` would now be available to our project. Unfortunately, that's not the case here; for iOS development, we need to tell Xcode about this library.

With your project open in Xcode, right-click on `Libraries`, then Add Files to "Depends"... (Figure 7-1).

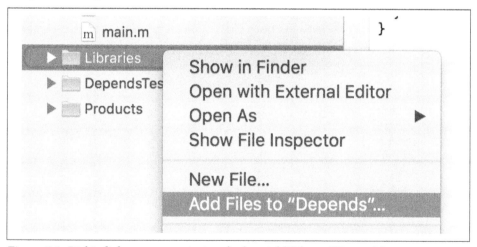

Figure 7-1. Right-click on your project and select Add Files to "Depends"...

Then add the *RCTVideo.xcodeproj* file to your project (Figure 7-2).

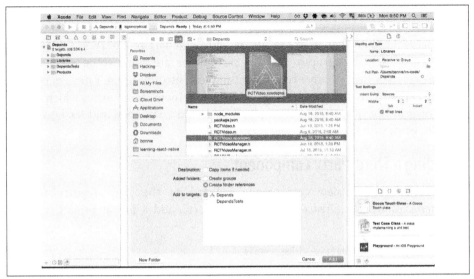

Figure 7-2. Select RCTVideo.xcodeproj from the list of files; it should be located under node_modules/react-native-video

You'll also have to add the video framework to your project's build process. Under Build Phases, go to the Link Binary With Libraries submenu, and click the "+" button. Then add *libRCTVideo.a* to your project (Figure 7-3).

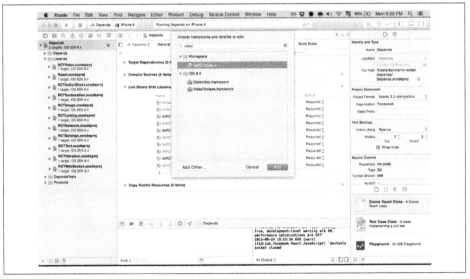

Figure 7-3. Add the libRCTVideo.a file (you can use the search bar to help you locate the correct file)

With that, you're done importing the RCTVideo module into your project! We also need to import our mp4 video file into our Xcode project, so that it is available as a resource. Right-click on your project and select Add Files to Depends again, as shown in Figure 7-4.

Any mp4 video file ought to work; I used a video of a past project, as I had it on hand. You can download it from GitHub (*http://bit.ly/1MH8JwT*).

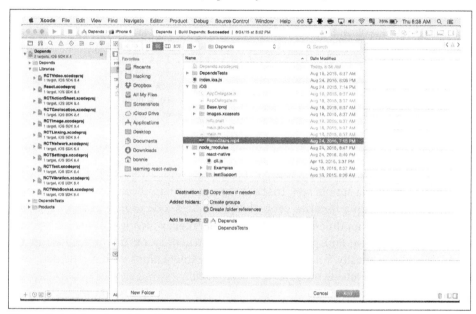

Figure 7-4. Select the video file you want to use; here, we're using PianoStairs.mp4

Afterward, you should see the video file in your project (Figure 7-5).

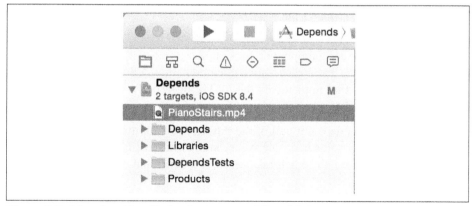

Figure 7-5. After the video file has been successfully added to your project, you should see it in Xcode

Using the Video Component

OK, now that you've imported it into Xcode, we can require the Video component from our JavaScript code:

```
var Video = require('react-native-video');
```

Then use the component, just as you normally would. Here I've set a few of the optional props:

```
<Video source={{uri: "PianoStairs"}} // Can be a URL or a local file.
       rate={1.0}                    // 0 is paused, 1 is normal.
       volume={1.0}                  // 0 is muted, 1 is normal.
       muted={false}                 // Mutes the audio entirely.
       paused={false}                // Pauses playback entirely.
       resizeMode="cover"            // Fill the whole screen at aspect ratio.
       repeat={true}                 // Repeat forever.
       style={styles.backgroundVideo} />
```

Ta-da! We have a working video component!

Though the process of using third-party modules with React Native is somewhat more involved than a simple npm install, it's not too bad. The most confusing part, potentially, is including libraries properly into your Xcode project and dealing with the Xcode GUI. For modules like react-native-video, which was developed specifically for React Native and provides detailed instructions on this procedure in the README, this is mostly a nonissue. Don't let the interactions with Xcode deter you from incorporating outside modules into your code!

Many such components are listed in the npm registry, and often use the prefix react-native-. Take a look around and see what the community has built!

Anatomy of an Objective-C Native Module

Now that we're using the react-native-video module, let's look at how modules like these work under the hood.

The react-native-video component is what React refers to as a native module (*http://bit.ly/1PVBCcZ*). The React Native documentation defines a *native module* as "an Objective-C class that implements the RCTBridgeModule protocol." (RCT is an abbreviation for ReaCT.)

Writing Objective-C code is not part of the standard development process with React Native, so don't worry—this is not necessary stuff! But having basic reading knowledge of what's going on will be helpful, even if you don't plan on implementing your own native modules (yet).

If you have never worked with Objective-C before, much of the syntax you'll encounter may seem confusing. That's OK! We'll take things slowly. Let's start by building a basic "Hello, World" module.

Objective-C classes usually have a header file that ends in .h, which contains the interface for a class. The actual implementation goes in a .m file. Let's start by writing our *HelloWorld.h* file, shown in Example 7-1.

Example 7-1. Depends/iOS/HelloWorld.h

```
#import "RCTBridgeModule.h"

@interface HelloWorld : NSObject <RCTBridgeModule>
@end
```

What does this file do? On the first line, we import the RCTBridgeModule header. (Note that the # symbol does *not* denote a comment, but rather an import statement.) Then, on the next line, we declare that the HelloWorld class subclasses NSObject and implements the RCTBridgeModule interface, and end the interface declaration with @end.

Due to historical reasons, many basic types in Objective-C are prefixed with NS (NSString, NSObject, etc.).

Now let's move on to the implemenation (Example 7-2).

Example 7-2. Depends/iOS/HelloWorld.m

```
#import "HelloWorld.h"
#import "RCTLog.h"

@implementation HelloWorld

RCT_EXPORT_MODULE();

RCT_EXPORT_METHOD(greeting:(NSString *)name)
{
  RCTLogInfo(@"Saluton, %@", name);
}

@end
```

In a .m file, you'll want to import the corresponding .h file, as we do here on the first line. I've also imported *RCTLog.h*, so that we can log things to the console using RCTLogInfo. When importing other classes in Objective-C, you'll almost always want to import the header file, *not* the .m file.

The @implementation and @end lines indicate that the contents between them are the implementation of the HelloWorld class.

The remaining lines do the work of making this a React Native module. With RCT_EXPORT_MODULE(), we invoke a special React Native macro that makes this class accessible to the React Native bridge. Similarly, our method definition for greeting:name is prefixed with a macro, RCT_EXPORT_METHOD, which exports the method and thus will expose it to our JavaScript code.

Note that Objective-C methods are named with a somewhat odd syntax. Each parameter's name is included in the method name. It's React Native convention that the JavaScript function name is the Objective-C name, up until the first colon, so greeting:name becomes greeting in JavaScript. You may use the macro RCT_REMAP_METHOD to remap this naming if you like.

We can then invoke the method from our JavaScript files (Example 7-3).

Example 7-3. Using the HelloWorld module from our JavaScript code

```
var HelloWorld = require('react-native').NativeModules.HelloWorld;
HelloWorld.greeting('Bonnie');
```

The output should appear in the console (Figure 7-6), both in Xcode and in the Chrome developer tools, if you choose to enable them.

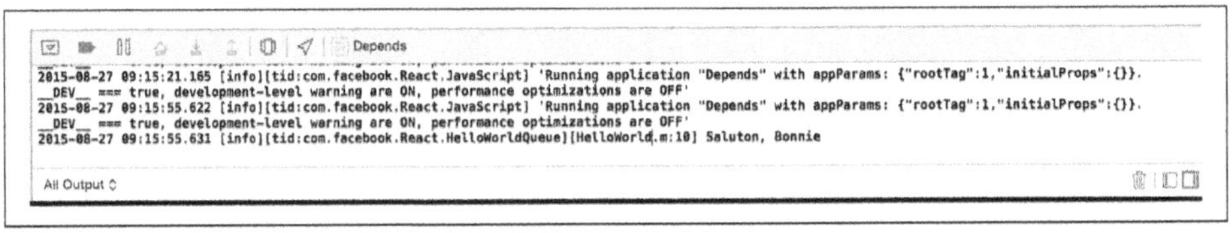

Figure 7-6. Console output, as viewed through the Xcode interface

Note that the syntax for importing native modules is a bit verbose. A common approach is to wrap your native module in a JavaScript module (Example 7-4).

Example 7-4. Depends/HelloWorld.js: a JavaScript wrapper for the HelloWorld native module

```
var HelloWorld = require('react-native').NativeModules.HelloWorld;
module.exports = HelloWorld;
```

Then, requiring it becomes much more straightforward:

```
var HelloWorld = require('./HelloWorld');
```

The *HelloWorld.js* JavaScript file is also a good opportunity to add any JavaScript-side functionality to your module.

Phew. Objective-C can feel verbose, and we have to keep track of a couple of different files. But congratulations—you've written a "Hello, World" for your Objective-C module!

To review, an Objective-C module must do the following in order to be available in React Native:

- Import the `RCTBridgeModule` header
- Declare that your module implements the `RCTBridgeModule` interface
- Call the `RCT_EXPORT_MODULE()` macro
- Have at least one method that is exported using the `RCT_EXPORT_METHOD` macro

Native modules can then make use of any API provided by the iOS SDK. (Note that the API you provide to React Native *must* be asynchronous.) Apple provides extensive documentation for the iOS SDK, and there are many resources available from third parties as well. Note that your developer licenses will come in handy here—it's often difficult to access the SDK documentation without one.

Now that we've written our own basic "Hello, World," let's take a deeper look at how `react-native-video` is implemented.

Implementation of RCTVideo

Just like our `HelloWorld` module, `RCTVideo` is a native module, and it implements the `RCTBridgeModule` protocol. You can see the full code for `RCTVideo` in the react-native-video GitHub repository (*https://github.com/brentvatne/react-native-video*). We'll be looking at version 0.6.0.

`react-native-video` is basically a wrapper around the `AVPlayer` API provided by the iOS SDK. Let's take a closer look at how it works, beginning with the JavaScript entry points *Video.ios.js* and *Video.android.js*. In this version, *Video.android.js* is still unimplemented, so let's look at Video.ios.js (*http://bit.ly/1MDYGsr*).

We can see that it provides a thin wrapper around the native component, `RCTVideo`, performing some props normalization and a bit of extra rendering logic. The native component is imported at the end:

```
var RCTVideo = requireNativeComponent('RCTVideo', Video);
```

As we saw in our `HelloWorld` example, that means that somewhere the `RCTVideo` component must be exported from Objective-C. Let's look at *RCTVideo.h* (*http://bit.ly/1Mp0k3e*):

```
// RCTVideo.h
#import "RCTView.h"
```

```
@class RCTEventDispatcher;

@interface RCTVideo : UIView

- (instancetype)initWithEventDispatcher:
(RCTEventDispatcher *)eventDispatcher NS_DESIGNATED_INITIALIZER;

@end
```

This time, instead of subclassing NSObject, RCTVideo subclasses UIView. That makes sense, because it's rendering a view component.

If we look at the implementation file, *RCTVideo.m* (*http://bit.ly/1HaVveX*), there's a *lot* going on. At the top are instance variables, keeping track of things like volume, playback rate, and the AVPlayer itself.

There's one interesting method, methodQueue, which we should look at:

```
- (dispatch_queue_t)methodQueue
{
  return dispatch_get_main_queue();
}
```

This tells it to use the iOS main queue, necessary because the module uses main-thread-only iOS APIs.

There are also various methods for things like calculating the duration of the video, loading in the video and setting it as the source, and more. Feel free to step through these methods and figure out what role they play.

The other piece of the puzzle is the RCTVideoManager. To create a native UI component, as opposed to just a module, we also need a view manager. As the name implies, while the view actually handles rendering logic and similar tasks, the view manager deals with other stuff (event handling, property exports, etc.). At a minimum, the view manager class needs to:

- Subclass RCTViewManager
- Use the RCT_EXPORT_MODULE() macro
- Implement the -(UIView *)view method

The view method should return a UIView instance. In this case, we can see that it instantiates and returns a RCTVideo:

```
- (UIView *)view
{
  return [[RCTVideo alloc] initWithEventDispatcher:self.bridge.eventDispatcher];
}
```

The RCTVideoManager also exports a number of properties and constants:

```
RCT_EXPORT_VIEW_PROPERTY(src, NSDictionary);
RCT_EXPORT_VIEW_PROPERTY(resizeMode, NSString);
RCT_EXPORT_VIEW_PROPERTY(repeat, BOOL);
RCT_EXPORT_VIEW_PROPERTY(paused, BOOL);
RCT_EXPORT_VIEW_PROPERTY(muted, BOOL);
RCT_EXPORT_VIEW_PROPERTY(volume, float);
RCT_EXPORT_VIEW_PROPERTY(rate, float);
RCT_EXPORT_VIEW_PROPERTY(seek, float);

- (NSDictionary *)constantsToExport
{
  return @{
    @"ScaleNone": AVLayerVideoGravityResizeAspect,
    @"ScaleToFill": AVLayerVideoGravityResize,
    @"ScaleAspectFit": AVLayerVideoGravityResizeAspect,
    @"ScaleAspectFill": AVLayerVideoGravityResizeAspectFill
  };
```

Together, `RCTVideo` and `RCTVideoManager` comprise the `RCTVideo` native UI component, which we can use freely from within our application. As you can see, writing native modules that make use of the iOS SDK is a nontrivial endeavor, though not an insurmountable one. This is definitely one area where previous iOS development experience will serve you well. A full explanation of iOS development is certainly beyond the scale of this book, but by looking at others' native modules, even if you don't have much Objective-C experience, you should be able to start experimenting with your own attempts at native module development.

Native Modules for Android

Native modules for Android behave similarly to native modules for iOS. You can find more information about Android native modules in the docs (*http://bit.ly/1kQ3STm*).

For this section, we'll work in the *AndroidDepends/* project directory. Go ahead and make a new project:

```
react-native init AndroidDepends
```

Installing a Third-Party Component

For this section, we'll install the `react-native-linear-gradient` package, which provides us with a `<LinearGradient>` component. Because creating gradients is a relatively graphics-heavy task, it makes sense to utilize native platform APIs for this component. So, `<LinearGradient>` provides a unified React Native component, which uses the `android.graphics` package and `CAGradientLayer` APIs under the hood for Android and iOS, respectively. You can find the project on GitHub (*https://github.com/brentvatne/react-native-linear-gradient*).

Like on iOS, installing native modules for Android requires us to touch the Android-specific project code. Generally speaking, to include a third-party Android native module, you'll need to do three things:

1. Update your *android/settings.gradle* so that the module is included in your Android build.

2. List the module as a dependency in *android/app/build.gradle*.

3. Import the package in *MainActivity.java* and include it as a package available to React Native.

Let's go through these one by one. First, we update *settings.gradle* to include the *react-native-linear-gradient* directory. The *settings.gradle* file should look like Example 7-5.

Example 7-5. AndroidDepends/android/settings.gradle

```
rootProject.name = 'AndroidDepends'

include ':app', ':react-native-linear-gradient'
project(':react-native-linear-gradient').projectDir =
  new File(rootProject.projectDir,
    '../node_modules/react-native-linear-gradient/android')
```

Gradle is a build system for Android. When we use `npm install` to install the `react-native-linear-gradient` package, the relevant Android-specific files get downloaded into our *node_modules/* folder. Updating *settings.gradle* includes that folder in our build.

Next, we need to list the `react-native-linear-gradient` module as a dependency in our *build.gradle* file (Example 7-6). You can see that this file includes a number of build settings, such as the target Android SDK version, as well as application dependencies, such as React Native. We need to add `react-native-linear-gradient` to the list of dependencies at the bottom of the file.

Example 7-6. AndroidDepends/android/app/build.gradle

```
apply plugin: 'com.android.application'

android {
    compileSdkVersion 23
    buildToolsVersion "23.0.1"

    defaultConfig {
        applicationId "com.androiddepends"
        minSdkVersion 16
        targetSdkVersion 22
        versionCode 1
```

```
        versionName "1.0"
        ndk {
            abiFilters "armeabi-v7a", "x86"
        }
    }
    buildTypes {
        release {
            minifyEnabled false
            proguardFiles getDefaultProguardFile('proguard-android.txt'),
            'proguard-rules.pro'
        }
    }
}

dependencies {
    compile fileTree(dir: 'libs', include: ['*.jar'])
    compile 'com.android.support:appcompat-v7:23.0.1'
    compile 'com.facebook.react:react-native:0.12.+'
    compile project(':react-native-linear-gradient')
}
```

Finally, we need to update our *MainActivity.java*. There are two steps here: importing the `LinearGradientPackage`, and then adding it to our `ReactInstanceManager`.

You can add the following import statement anywhere at the top of the file, as long as it's before the class declaration:

```
import com.BV.LinearGradient.LinearGradientPackage;
```

Then, add the package to your `ReactInstanceManager`, by adding another `addPackage()` call after the existing one:

```
mReactInstanceManager = ReactInstanceManager.builder()
        .setApplication(getApplication())
        .setBundleAssetName("index.android.bundle")
        .setJSMainModuleName("index.android")
        .addPackage(new MainReactPackage())
        .addPackage(new LinearGradientPackage()) // Add this line!
        .setUseDeveloperSupport(BuildConfig.DEBUG)
        .setInitialLifecycleState(LifecycleState.RESUMED)
        .build();
```

OK! After you do that, we can import the package from our JavaScript code like so:

```
var LinearGradient = require('react-native-linear-gradient');
```

Then we can use the component from React Native:

```
<LinearGradient colors={['#FFFFFF', '#00A8A8']} style={styles.container}>
  <Text style={styles.welcome}>
    A Lovely Gradient
  </Text>
</LinearGradient>
```

Let's use this to make a new <Gradient> component, to replace the default application screen (Example 7-7).

Example 7-7. AndroidDepends/gradient.js

```
var React = require('react-native');
var {
  StyleSheet,
  Text
} = React;
var LinearGradient = require('react-native-linear-gradient');

var Gradient = React.createClass({
  render: function() {
    return (
        <LinearGradient colors={['#FFFFFF', '#00A8A8']} style={styles.container}>
          <Text style={styles.welcome}>
            A Lovely Gradient
          </Text>
        </LinearGradient>
    );
  }
});

var styles = StyleSheet.create({
  container: {
    flex: 1,
    justifyContent: 'center',
    alignItems: 'center'
  },
  welcome: {
    fontSize: 20,
    textAlign: 'center',
    margin: 10,
    height: 50,
    padding: 20
  }
});

module.exports = Gradient;
```

And that should be all we need to make use of the <LinearGradient> component. Change your *index.android.js* file to render the <Gradient> component. It should render a gradient with some text, as shown in Figure 7-7.

Figure 7-7. The <Gradient> component

Cool! Now that we've covered how to include a third-party native module for Android, we'll look at how native modules in general work by building another "Hello, World" module, but this time in Java instead of Objective-C. After that, we can take a closer look at how `react-native-linear-gradient` works.

Anatomy of a Java Native Module

In order to better understand how Java native modules work, we'll write our own. Just like with Objective-C, we'll start with a simpe "Hello, World" module.

We'll begin by adding a *HelloWorld.java* file (Example 7-8). Remember that Android projects have a pretty deep nesting structure. Let's make *HelloWorld.java* a sibling to our *MainActivity.java* file.

Example 7-8. AndroidDepends/android/app/src/main/java/com/androiddepends/HelloWorld.java

```
package com.androiddepends;

import com.facebook.react.bridge.NativeModule;
import com.facebook.react.bridge.ReactApplicationContext;
import com.facebook.react.bridge.ReactContext;
import com.facebook.react.bridge.ReactContextBaseJavaModule;
import com.facebook.react.bridge.ReactMethod;

import android.util.Log;

public class HelloWorld extends ReactContextBaseJavaModule {

  public HelloWorld(ReactApplicationContext reactContext) {
    super(reactContext);
  }

  @Override
  public String getName() {
    return "HelloWorld";
  }

  @ReactMethod
  public void greeting(String name) {
    Log.i("HelloWorld", "Hello, " + name);
  }
}
```

There's quite a bit of boilerplate here! Let's take this piece by piece.

First, we begin with a package statement:

```
package com.androiddepends;
```

All source files in the `com.androiddepends` package must begin with this line. We're using the same package as our *MainActivity.java* file for convenience's sake.

Next, we import a bunch of React Native-specific files, as well as *android.util.Log*. Any module you write should import the same React Native files.

Then, we declare our `HelloWorld` class. It's public, meaning that external files can use it; and it extends the `ReactContextBaseJavaModule`, meaning that it inherits methods from `ReactContextBaseJavaModule`:

```
public class HelloWorld extends ReactContextBaseJavaModule { ... }
```

There are three methods implemented here: `HelloWorld`, `getName`, and `greeting`.

In Java, a method with the same name as the class is called the *constructor*. The `Hello World` method is thus a bit of boilerplate; we invoke the `ReactContextBase JavaModule` constructor with a call to `super(reactContext)` and don't do anything else.

`getName` determines which name we'll use later on to access this module from our JavaScript code, so make sure it's correct! In this case, we name it "HelloWorld." Note that we add an `@Override` decorator here. You'll want to implement `getName` for any other modules you write.

Finally, `greeting` is our own method, which we want to be available in our JavaScript code. We add a `@ReactMethod` decorator so that React Native knows this method should be exposed. To log something when `greeting` is called, we call `Log.i` like so:

```
Log.i("HelloWorld", "Hello, " + name);
```

The `Log` object in Android provides different levels of logging. The three most commonly used are INFO, WARN, and ERROR, and are invoked with `Log.i`, `Log.w`, and `Log.e`, respectively. Each of these methods takes in two parameters: the "tag" for your log, and the message. It's standard practice to use the class name for the tag. View the Android documentation (*http://bit.ly/1MxTUiq*) for more details.

We also need to create a Package file to wrap this module (Example 7-9), so that we can include it in our build. It should also be a sibling to *HelloWorld.java*.

Example 7-9. AndroidDepends/android/app/src/main/java/com/androiddepends/ HelloWorldPackage.java

```
package com.androiddepends;

import com.facebook.react.ReactPackage;
import com.facebook.react.bridge.JavaScriptModule;
import com.facebook.react.bridge.NativeModule;
import com.facebook.react.bridge.ReactApplicationContext;
import com.facebook.react.uimanager.ViewManager;

import java.util.ArrayList;
import java.util.Collections;
import java.util.List;

public class HelloWorldPackage implements ReactPackage {
```

```
@Override
public List<NativeModule>
createNativeModules(ReactApplicationContext reactContext) {
  List<NativeModule> modules = new ArrayList<>();
  modules.add(new HelloWorld(reactContext));
  return modules;
}

public List<Class<? extends JavaScriptModule>> createJSModules() {
  return Collections.emptyList();
}

public List<ViewManager> createViewManagers(ReactApplicationContext reactContext) {
  return Collections.emptyList();
}
}
```

This file is mostly boilerplate. We don't need to import HelloWorld because it's part of the same package (com.androiddepends) as this file. There are three methods here worth noting: createNativeModules, createJSModules, and createViewManagers. React Native uses these methods to determine what modules it should export.

In this case, we only wrote a so-called native module, so the latter two methods return an empty list, while createNativeModules returns a list containing an instance of HelloWorld. By contrast, if you look at *LinearGradientPackage.java* (source (*http://bit.ly/215jRxn*)), you'll see that it returns an instance of LinearGra dientManager in the call to createViewManagers and empty lists for the other two methods.

Finally, we need to add the package in *MainActivity.java*, just like we did with LinearGradient. Import the package file:

```
import com.androiddepends.HelloWorldPackage;
```

Then add HelloWorldPackage to your ReactInstanceManager:

```
mReactInstanceManager = ReactInstanceManager.builder()
        .setApplication(getApplication())
        .setBundleAssetName("index.android.bundle")
        .setJSMainModuleName("index.android")
        .addPackage(new MainReactPackage())
        .addPackage(new LinearGradientPackage())
        .addPackage(new HelloWorldPackage()) // <-- Add this line
        .setUseDeveloperSupport(BuildConfig.DEBUG)
        .setInitialLifecycleState(LifecycleState.RESUMED)
        .build();
```

Just like with Objective-C modules, our Java module will be available via the `React.NativeModules` object. We can now invoke our `greeting()` method from anywhere within our app like so:

```
React.NativeModules.HelloWorld.greeting("Bonnie");
```

Let's filter the logs and look for our message. Run the following from your project's root:

```
adb logcat | grep HelloWorld
```

We're searching for instances of "HelloWorld" because that's the tag we used in our call to `Log.i`. Figure 7-8 shows the output you should see in your shell.

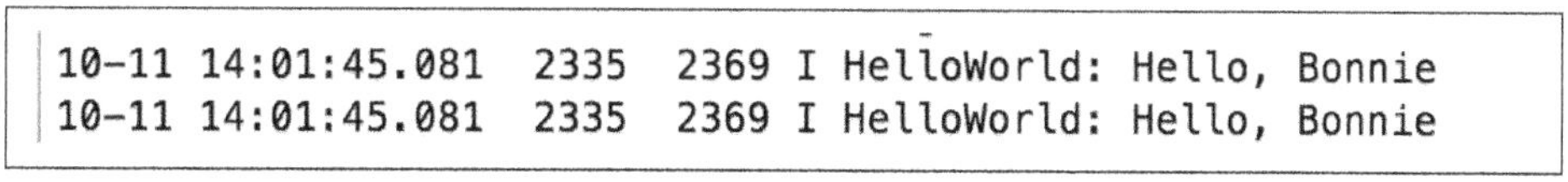

```
10-11 14:01:45.081   2335   2369 I HelloWorld: Hello, Bonnie
10-11 14:01:45.081   2335   2369 I HelloWorld: Hello, Bonnie
```

Figure 7-8. Output from logcat

Now that we've written our "Hello, World" example from Java, let's look at the implementation of a more complex example: `react-native-linear-gradient`.

Android Implementation of LinearGradient

The Android implementation of `<LinearGradient>` is located in the *android/* directory (*https://github.com/brentvatne/react-native-linear-gradient/tree/master/android*). It consists primarily of three files:

- *LinearGradientPackage.java*
- *LinearGradientView.java*
- *LinearGradientManager.java*

LinearGradientPackage.java, shown in Example 7-10, looks extremely similar to our *HelloWorldPackage.java* file.

Example 7-10. LinearGradientPackage.java

```
package com.BV.LinearGradient;

import com.facebook.react.ReactPackage;
import com.facebook.react.bridge.JavaScriptModule;
import com.facebook.react.bridge.NativeModule;
import com.facebook.react.bridge.ReactApplicationContext;
import com.facebook.react.uimanager.ViewManager;

import java.util.ArrayList;
import java.util.Collections;
```

```
import java.util.List;

public class LinearGradientPackage implements ReactPackage {

  @Override
  public List<NativeModule>
  createNativeModules(ReactApplicationContext reactContext) {
    return Collections.emptyList();
  }

  public List<Class<? extends JavaScriptModule>> createJSModules() {
    return Collections.emptyList();
  }

  public List<ViewManager> createViewManagers(ReactApplicationContext reactContext) {
    List<ViewManager> modules = new ArrayList<>();
    modules.add(new LinearGradientManager());
    return modules;
  }
}
```

The main difference is that `LinearGradientPackage` returns `LinearGradi
entManager` from `createViewManagers`, while our `HelloWorldPackage` returned
`HelloWorld` from `createNativeModules`. What's the difference?

For Android, any natively rendering views are created and controlled by a
`ViewManager` (or, more specifically, a class that extends `ViewManager`). Because `Lin
earGradient` is a UI component, we need to return a `ViewManager`. The React Native
documentation on native Android UI components (*https://facebook.github.io/react-
native/docs/native-components-android.html*) has some more information on the difference between exposing a native module (i.e., nonrendering Java code) and a UI
component.

Let's look at `LinearGradientManager` next. It's a relatively long file; you can view the
full source in the react-native-linear-gradient GitHub repo (*https://github.com/brent
vatne/react-native-linear-gradient*). We'll look at an abbreviated version here:

```
public class LinearGradientManager extends SimpleViewManager<FrameLayout> {

    ...

    public static final String REACT_CLASS = "BVLinearGradient";
    public static final String PROP_COLORS = "colors";
    public LinearGradientView mGradientView;

    ...

    @Override
    public String getName() {
        return REACT_CLASS;
```

```
    }

    ...

    @ReactProp(name=PROP_COLORS)
    public void updateColors(FrameLayout frame, ReadableArray colors){
        if(mGradientView != null) {
            mGradientView.updateColors(colors);
        }
    }

    ...

    @Override
    public void updateView(FrameLayout frame, CatalystStylesDiffMap props) {
        BaseViewPropertyApplicator.applyCommonViewProperties(frame, props);

        frame.removeAllViews();

        mGradientView = new LinearGradientView(frame.getContext(), props);
        mGradientView.setId(View.generateViewId());

        frame.addView(mGradientView);
    }
}
```

There are a few things we should pay attention to here.

The first is the implementation of getName. Note that, just as in our HelloWorld example, we need to implement getName in order to be able to refer to this component from our JavaScript code!

The next is the updateColors method, and the use of the @ReactProp decorator. Here we declare that the <LinearGradient> component will take a prop named colors (as that's the value of PROP_COLORS), and updateColors will be invoked when that prop changes. In updateColors, we check to see that the underlying view exists; if it does, we pass the colors along so that it can update.

Finally, in updateView, LinearGradientManager handles actually updating the view, by removing any existing views from the frame and then adding a new instance of LinearGradientView to the frame.

In order to effectively write native Android components, you'll want an understanding of how Android handles Views in general, but looking at other React Native components is a good place to start.

Cross-Platform Native Modules

Is it possible to write a cross-platform native module?

The answer is "yes"; you just have to implement your module separately for each platform, and provide a unified JavaScript interface. This can be a good way to handle platform-specific optimizations while still maximizing code reuse.

The <LinearGradient> component is a good example of this. Our AndroidDepends project is actually cross-platform, because <LinearGradient> renders cross-platform (albeit with a few style differences); see Figure 7-9.

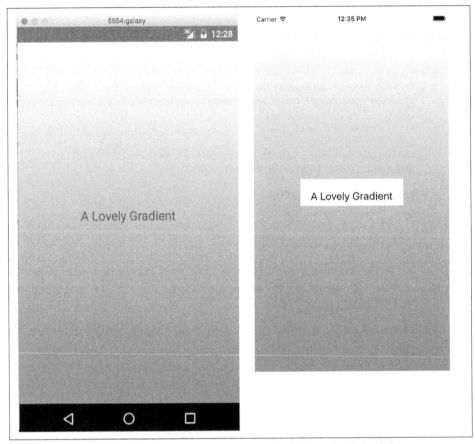

Figure 7-9. The <Gradient> component, on Android (left) and iOS (right)

Creating a cross-platform native module is pretty simple and doesn't require much extra configuration. Once you have implemented iOS and Android versions separately, just create a folder containing *index.ios.js* and *index.android.js* files. Each version should require the appropriate native module. Then you can require that folder, and React Native will pick up the platform-appropriate version.

For instance, the *react-native-linear-gradient/* folder (in our *node_modules/* directory, as we installed it via npm) contains an *index.ios.js* and an *index.android.js* file. React

Native will pick up the appropriate file for us—we just need to require the *react-native-linear-gradient/* folder like so:

```
var LinearGradient = require('react-native-linear-gradient');
```

As it currently stands, React Native won't enforce a consistent API between the iOS and Android versions, so that responsibility falls on you. If you want the iOS and Android versions to have slightly different APIs, that's fine, too!

Summary

So, when is it appropriate to use native Objective-C or Java code? When is it a good idea to include third-party modules and libraries? In general, there are three main use cases for native modules: taking advantage of existing Objective-C or Java code; writing high-performance, multithreaded code for tasks such as graphics processing; and exposing APIs not yet included in React Native.

For any existing mobile projects built in Objective-C or Java, writing a native module can be a great way to reuse existing code in React Native applications. While hybrid applications are a bit beyond the scope of this book, they're definitely a feasible approach, and you can use native modules to share functionality between JavaScript, Objective-C, and Java.

Similarly, for use cases where performance is critical, or for specialized tasks, it often makes sense to work in the native langague of the platform you're developing for. In these cases, it often makes more sense to do the heavy lifting in Objective-C or Java, and then pass the result back to your JavaScript application.

Finally, there will inevitably be platform APIs you'll want to use that aren't yet supported by React Native. React Native is under active development, and support for any given platform will almost certainly *always* be incomplete. In these cases, you have two options. One is to turn to the community, and hope that someone else has already solved your problem. The alternative is to solve the issue yourself, and hopefully contribute your solution back to the community! Being able to write your own native modules means that you don't need to rely on React Native core in order to take advantage of your host platform.

Even if you've never developed for iOS or Android before, if you're planning on developing with React Native, it's a good idea to try and gain a reading knowledge of Objective-C and/or Java. Just in case you hit a wall when working with React Native, being able to try and dig your way around it is a really invaluable asset, and native modules are actually fairly approachable. Don't be afraid to try!

The React Native community, as well as the broader JavaScript ecosystem, will be valuable assets as you develop your own React Native applications. Build on the work of others, and reach out if you need help!

Debugging and Developer Tools

As you develop your own applications, chances are that *something* will go wrong along the way. When it's time to debug your applications, we happily have some React Native-specific tools that will make the job easier. There are also some nasty bugs that can crop up at the intersection of React Native and its host platform, which we'll take a look at, too. In this chapter, we'll dig into common pitfalls of React Native development, and the tools you can use to tackle them. And because any discussion of debugging would be incomplete without reference to testing, we'll also cover the basics of getting automated testing set up for your React Native code.

JavaScript Debugging Practices, Translated

When working with React for the Web, we have a number of common JavaScript-based tools and techniques to help us debug our applications. Most of these are also available for React Native, though occasionally with some minor adjustments. React Native gives us access to the console, debugger, and React developer tools that we're accustomed to using, so debugging JavaScript-based issues in React Native should feel familiar.

Activating the Developer Options

In order to avail yourself of these tools, you'll need to enable Chrome Developer Tools in the in-app developer menu (Figure 8-1). This menu can be accessed by pressing Command+Control+Z in the iOS simulator, pressing the hardware button on Android, or by shaking your device. From there, you can select Debug in Chrome to enable the Chrome Developer Tools.

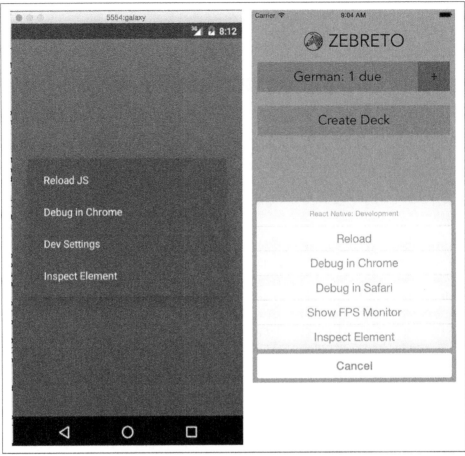

Figure 8-1. The in-app developer menu, as viewed from Android (left) and iOS (right)

Debugging with console.log

One of the most basic, and common, forms of debugging is the "print it out and see what's happening" tactic. For many web-based developers, being able to add console.log to our code is an almost unconscious part of our workflow.

The JavaScript console works straight out of the box with React Native; you don't need to do any special configuration in order to use your print statements.

When using Xcode, you will see your console statements as output in the Xcode console (Figure 8-2). Note that you can expand how much room is allotted to the console by tweaking the visible Xcode panes.

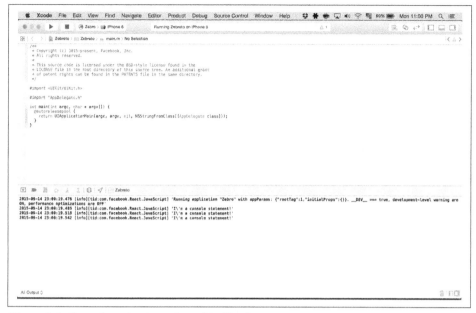

Figure 8-2. Console output, as viewed in Xcode

Similarly, for Android, you can view the logs for your device by running logcat from your project's root (Figure 8-3 shows the output):

```
adb logcat
```

```
10-11 20:12:10.139  2070  2085 E Surface : getSlotFromBufferLocked: unknown buffer: 0xab751700
10-11 20:12:10.368  1282  1301 W AppOps  : Finishing op nesting under-run: uid 10058 pkg com.androiddepends code 24 time=0 duration=0 nesting=0
10-11 20:12:10.440  2070  2104 W ReactNativeJS: 'Warning: Native component for "RCTModalHostView" does not exist'
10-11 20:12:10.528  2070  2104 D ReactNativeJS: 'Running application "AndroidDepends" with appParams: {"initialProps":{},"rootTag":1}. __DEV__ === true, devel
opment-level warning are ON, performance optimizations are OFF'
10-11 20:12:10.530  1282  1293 W InputMethodManagerService: Window already focused, ignoring focus gain of: com.android.internal.view.IInputMethodClient$Stub$
Proxy@c707531 attribute=null, token = android.os.BinderProxy@e14e28e
10-11 20:12:10.542  2070  2104 D ReactNativeJS: 'CONSOLE.LOG IN LOGCAT'
```

Figure 8-3. Console output appears with the tag of "ReactNativeJS" in logcat

However, these views are rather cluttered, and also include logging related to platform-specific things. We can hop over into the browser-based developer tools instead. Activate the developer menu and select Debug in Chrome, and then open your console. As shown in Figure 8-4, you will be able to see the console output from the Chrome developer tools.

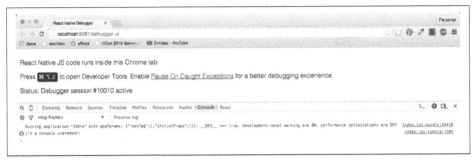

Figure 8-4. Console output, as viewed in Chrome

Note that you need to open the console before you'll see things appear here.

How does this work? When you load your React Native application with Chrome debugging enabled, Google Chrome loads your React Native JavaScript code from the React Native Packager using a standard `<script>` tag, so that you have full browser-based debugging control. The Packager then uses WebSockets to communicate commands between the device and the browser.

We don't need to be too concerned with the specifics; we just need to know how to take advantage of these tools!

Using the JavaScript Debugger

You can also use the JavaScript debugger, just as you normally would for web-based React development. Open up the developer tools in Chrome, switch to the "source" tab, and then your breakpoints will be activated. You can see this in action in Figure 8-5.

Note that, similar to the JavaScript console, if you don't already have the developer tools pane open, the debugger may not be activated on your breakpoints. Likewise, if you don't have Debug in Chrome enabled, the debugger will not be activated.

Figure 8-5. Using the debugger

When using the debugger, you have access to the usual view of your source code from within Chrome, and you can interact with the current JavaScript context via the in-browser console as well.

Working with the React Developer Tools

When developing with React for the Web, the React Developer Tools are quite useful. They allow you to inspect the component hierarchy, examine the props and state of components, and modify the state from your browser. The React Developer Tools are available as a Chrome extension (*http://bit.ly/1O5DTlX*).

The React Developer Tools work with React Native as well, though the experience is somewhat different. After opening the developer tools, you'll need to interact briefly with your application in order for the bridge to attach (a simple tap or click on the screen should suffice); see Figures 8-6 and 8-7.

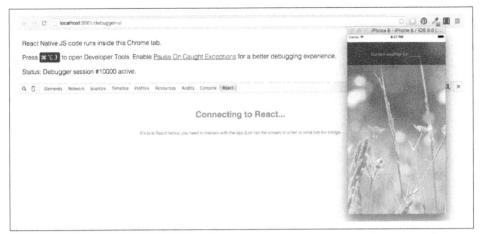

Figure 8-6. The view before the developer tools are attached (you need to tap on the screen)

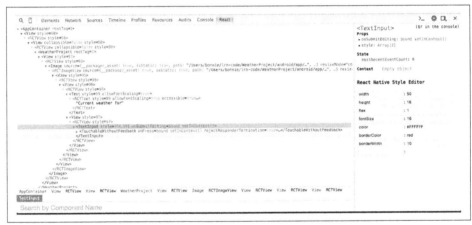

Figure 8-7. Viewing components and properties using the React Developer Tools

There are some limitations to these tools with React Native. The developer tools for Native are a work in progress, so not all features are fully fleshed out. The ability to edit styles from the inspector, for instance, is still somewhat fragile.

Another thing to watch out for is the lack of a `displayName` on many components. With React for the Web, you can usually set a component's `displayName` implicitly, like so:

```
import React from 'react';
var ComponentName = React.createClass({
    ...
});
```

```
export default ComponentName;
```

If you define your components like this, then you'll find that they're named properly when you inspect them with the React Developer Tools. Because this doesn't work with React Native, you should set the `displayName` explicitly instead:

```
import React from 'react-native';
var ComponentName = React.createClass({
  displayName: 'ComponentName'
  ...
});

export default ComponentName;
```

Once you've done so, the React Developer Tools will be able to parse your component hierarchy with well-labeled components as usual.

React Native Debugging Tools

In addition to the usual JavaScript-based web debugging tools, there are also some features specific to React Native that are relevant to debugging.

Using Inspect Element

While you can use the React developer tools via the browser, you may find that the "inspect element" functionality leaves something to be desired. There's also an in-app "inspect element" that you may find helpful. It has support for viewing things like style, and gives you a quick way to dig through the component hierarchy. In Figure 8-8, you can see the result of inspecting a button component.

Figure 8-8. Using Inspect Element will let you click on a component to view more information

This view also displays some basic performance metrics.

The Red Screen of Death

One of the most common sights you'll see during application development is the Red Screen of Death. Alarming appearance aside, the Red Screen of Death is actually a boon: it takes errors and parses them into meaningful messages. As such, learning to parse the information it displays is critical to an effective developer workflow.

For example, a syntax error might produce the output shown in Figure 8-9, indicating the file and line number where the error occurred.

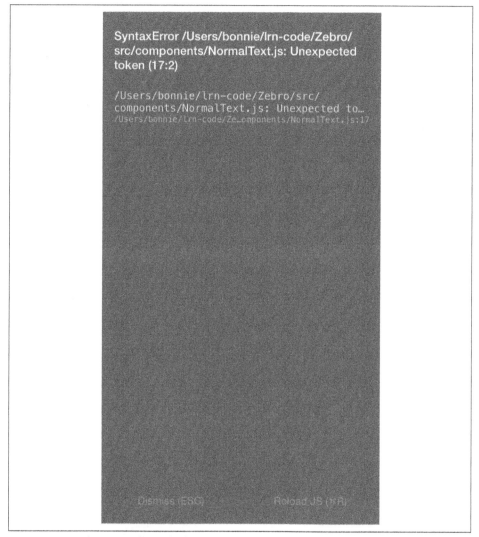

Figure 8-9. Red Screen of Death, for a syntax error

Other common errors include attempting to use a variable without importing or defining it. For instance, a common issue is failing to explicitly import the <Text> component, like so:

```
import React from 'react-native';

export default React.createClass({
```

```
  render() {
    return (
      <View>
        <Text>
          I haven't required things properly!
        </Text>
      </View>
    );
  }
})
```

This results in the error message shown in Figure 8-10:

Figure 8-10. Error message from forgetting to import Text

Attempting to use an undeclared variable results in another error message (see Figure 8-11).

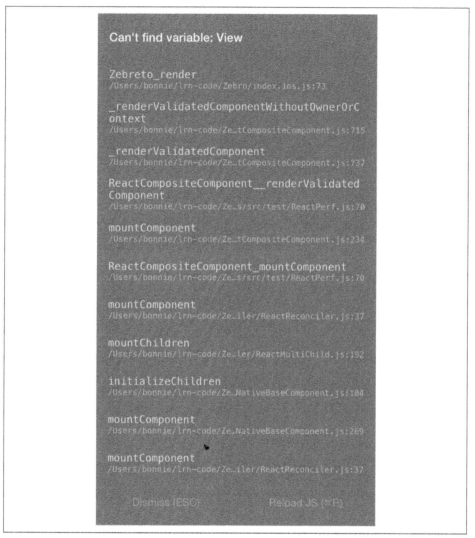

Figure 8-11. Error message from attempting to use an undeclared variable

Of particular use are the style-related error messages. For instance, if you pass in a bad value to a `StyleSheet.create` call, React Native will helpfully inform you which values would have been appropriate (see Figure 8-12).

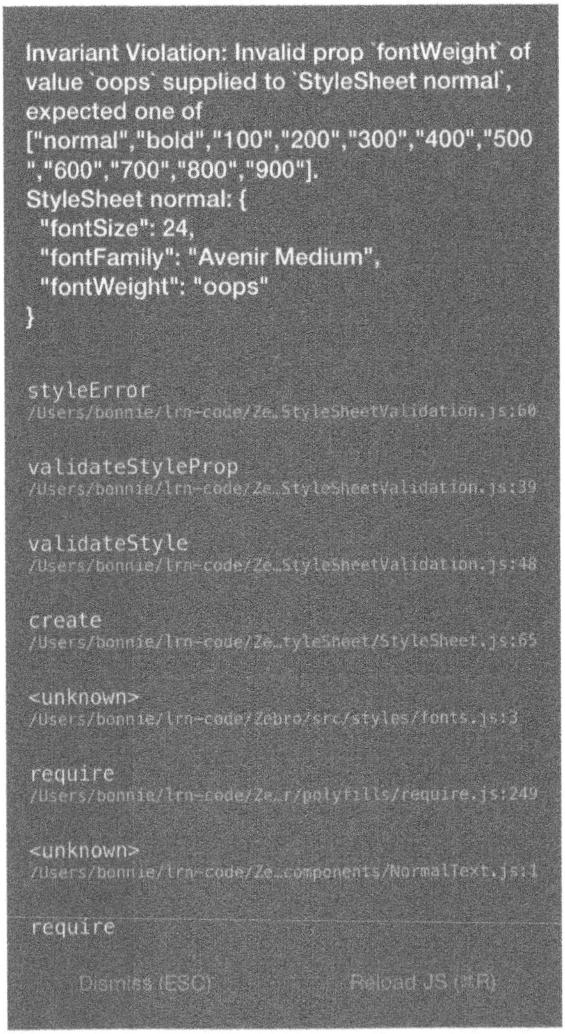

Figure 8-12. Error message from missetting a style property

While the Red Screen of Death may look alarming, it's really there to help you, and the error messages it presents are useful information. If for some reason you need to dismiss the screen, pressing the Escape key in the device simulator will take you back to your application.

Debugging Beyond JavaScript

As you write mobile applications with React Native, you will encounter errors not only in your React code, but also in your application in general. If you are new to mobile development, these issues can be frustrating. Additionally, sometimes you'll see cryptic error messages and issues where your JavaScript codebase meets the host platform; the combination of host platform code and React Native can lead to confusing symptoms.

Learning to debug issues outside of pure JavaScript-based problems is critical to a productive development process with React Native. Happily, many of these issues are simpler than they might seem at first glance, and we have plenty of tools to help us along the way.

Common Development Environment Issues

React Native is evolving quickly, which means that managing your developer environment can be a bit annoying.

If you encounter issues with the Packager starting, or with building or running your application using `npm start` or `react-native run-android`, it's possible that you have a dependency problem.

As always, if you're using brew to manage your dependencies, it's a good idea to keep brew up to date:

```
brew update
brew upgrade
```

When upgrading React Native, it's a good idea to run those brew commands, and then upgrade your node install as well:

```
brew upgrade node
```

Additionally, you can run `brew doctor` to check for issues with your installed packages.

If you're having dependency issues, another common solution is just to clean out your installed npm packages and reinstall them:

```
rm -rf node_modules
npm install
```

Common Xcode Problems

When you build your iOS application, if your application has any errors, they will appear in the Issues pane in Xcode (Figure 8-13). You can view them by selecting the warning icon.

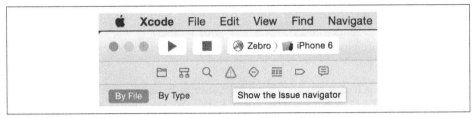

Figure 8-13. Viewing the issues pane

Xcode will then point you to the relevant file and line number, and highlight the issue in the IDE. Figure 8-14 shows an example of a common error.

```
// jsCodeLocation = [[NSBundle mainBundle] URLForResource:@"main" withExtension:@"jsbundle"];

RCTRootView *rootView = [[RCTRootView alloc] initWithBundleURL:jsCodeLocation
                        moduleName:@"Zebro"   No visible @interface for 'RCTRootView' declares the selector 'initWithBundleURL:moduleName:launchOptions'
                        launchOptions:launchOptions];
```

Figure 8-14. Interface error

This "No visible interface for RCTRootView" issue indicates that React Native's Objective-C classes are for some reason not visible to Xcode. In general, if you encounter "X is undefined" error messages in Xcode, where X is an RCT-prefixed class or otherwise part of React Native, it's a good idea to check on the packager, and to make sure that your JavaScript dependencies are in order:

1. Quit the packager
2. Quit Xcode
3. Run `npm install` from the project directory
4. Reopen Xcode

Another common problem deals with asset sizes (see Figure 8-15).

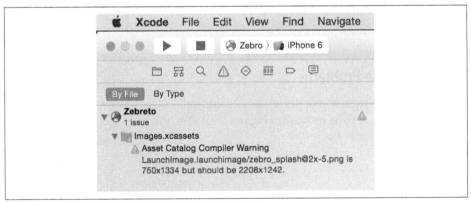

Figure 8-15. Warning regarding a missized image

Because assets should be sized appropriately for the device they're intended for (especially your application's icon), Xcode will throw a warning if you include an asset of an inappropriate size.

Deciphering Xcode's warnings may take some time at first, especially if you are unfamiliar with Objective-C. Some of the most confusing issues deal with the integration of React Native and your Xcode project, but doing a clean install of React Native usually clears up any problems.

Common Android Problems

When you run `react-native run-android`, some error messages may appear, preventing you from loading your application.

The two most common issues are typically missing Android dependencies, or a failure to boot an Android Virtual Device (or plug in an eligible device via USB).

If you receive a warning about a missing package, run `android` and check to see if that package is listed as "installed." If not, install it. If it *is* installed, but React Native can't find it, follow the steps above to try and fix any issues with your development environment. You should also check to make sure that your `ANDROID_HOME` environment variable is properly set and points to your installation of the Android SDK. For example, on my system:

```
$ echo $ANDROID_HOME
/usr/local/opt/android-sdk
```

If you receive a warning about no eligible device being available as a build target, check your device. Did you attempt to launch the emulator? If not, run `android avd`, and start an appropriate emulator. If the emulator is still booting, the `react-native run-android` command will fail; give it a few seconds and try again. If you're using a physical device, make sure that USB debugging is enabled.

You may also see issues after you create a signed version of your Android app, which we'll cover in Chapter 11:

```
$./gradlew installRelease
...
INSTALL_PARSE_FAILED_INCONSISTENT_CERTIFICATES:
New package has a different signature
```

This can be solved by uninstalling the old application from your device or emulator, and reattempting the installation. The error is caused by attempting to install an application with a different signing key—which of course happens after you generate your first signed APK.

The React Native Packager

Because React Native depends on the packager in order to rebuild your code, issues with the packager will manifest in problems fairly quickly.

The React Native packager will launch automatically when you run your project, either from Xcode or using `react-native run-android`. However, it will not quit automatically when you close your project. This means that if you switch projects, the packager will still be running—just from the wrong directory, so it will fail to compile your code. Always make sure that the packager is running from your project's root directory. You can launch it yourself with `npm start`.

If the React Native packager throws strange errors upon starting, chances are good that your development environment is in a bad state. Following the steps just described, make sure that your local installations of npm, node, and react-native are all in a good state.

Issues Deploying to an iOS Device

When attempting to test your application on a real iOS device, you may encounter some peculiar issues.

If you are having trouble uploading to your iOS device, the first thing you should do is check that your Apple Developer account is in order. Head to iTunes Connect (*http://itunesconnect.apple.com*) to check, and to accept any pending agreements. Without an Apple Developer account, you will not be able to deploy to a device.

Then, make sure that your device is selected correctly as the build target. Is your device of a supported type, based on your project settings? If your app explicitly disallows iPads, for instance, you won't be able to deploy to an iPad.

If you are using the React Packager to rebuild your files as you make edits, you may see the screen shown in Figure 8-16.

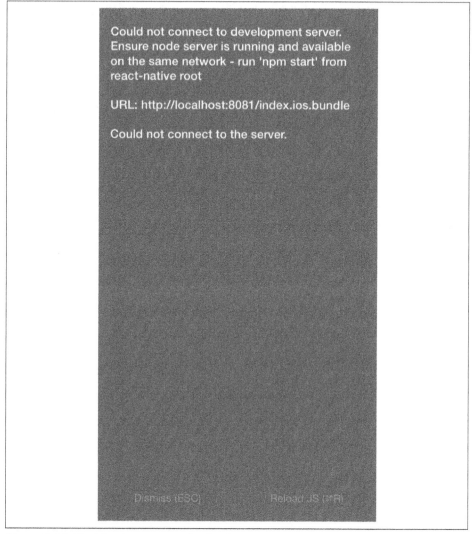

Figure 8-16. Could not connect to the development server

This indicates that your application has attempted to load its bundled JavaScript file from the React Native packager, but is unable to do so. In this case, run through the following checks:

- Are you using the packager option in *AppDelegate.m*?
- Is your IP address correct in *AppDelegate.m*?
- Are your computer and iOS device on the same WiFi network?
- Is the React Native packager running from the project directory?

- Can you access *http://your.ip.address:8081/index.ios.bundle* from your computer's browser?
- Can you access the same page from your iOS device's browser?

If you are using a prebuilt bundle of files, you may encounter a separate issue, where the default `react-native bundle --minify` command places your bundle in the wrong location. This is easily fixed by moving the *main.jsbundle* file to its appropriate path, based on the error message.

Simulator Behavior

You may also see strange behavior in the device simulator from time to time. If your application continues to crash repeatedly, or it seems like changes to your code are not being reflected on the simulator, the easiest first step is to delete your application from the device.

Note that simply deleting your application may not have the desired effect; on many systems, your app may leave behind files that can cause side effects later on. As shown in Figure 8-17, the most straightforward way to start over with a clean slate is to reset the device simulator entirely, which removes *all* files and applications from the simulated device.

Figure 8-17. The Reset Content and Settings... option will delete everything from your device

Testing Your Code

Debugging is all well and good, but you'll also want to prevent errors *before* they arise (and catch them when they inevitably do!). Automated tests and static type-checking are useful tools that you'll probably want to make use of in your applications.

Testing JavaScript Code

Much of the React Native code you write may not even be aware that it's running in a mobile environment. For example, any business logic can probably be isolated from rendering logic. That means that you can test your JavaScript code using whatever tools you prefer for ordinary JavaScript development. Woot!

In this section, we're going to look specifically at type-checking with Flow and unit-testing with Jest.

Type-Checking with Flow

Flow (*http://flowtype.org/*) is a JavaScript library for static type-checking. It relies on type inference to detect type errors even in unannotated code, and allows you to slowly add type annotations to existing projects. Type checking can help you detect possible issues early, and helps you enforce sane APIs between various components and modules.

Running Flow is simple:

```
$ flow check
```

The default application comes with a *.flowconfig* file, which configures Flow's behavior. If you see many errors related to files in `node_modules`, you may need to add this line to your *.flowconfig* under [`ignore`]:

```
.*/node_modules/.*
```

You should then be able to run `flow check` without seeing any errors:

```
$ flow check
$ Found 0 errors.
```

Feel free to use Flow to assist you as you develop your React Native applications.

Testing with Jest

React Native supports testing of React components using Jest. Jest is a unit testing framework built on top of Jasmine. It provides aggressive automocking of dependencies, and it meshes nicely with React's testing utilities.

To use Jest, you will first need to install it:

```
npm install jest-cli --save-dev
```

Update your *package.json* file to include a test script:

```
{
  ...
  "scripts": {
    "test": "jest"
  }
  ...
}
```

This will run jest when you type npm test.

Next, create the *tests/* directory. Jest will recursively search for files in a *tests/* directory, and run them:

```
mkdir __tests__
```

Now let's create a new file, *tests/dummy-test.js*, and write our first test:

```
'use strict';

describe('a silly test', function() {
 it('expects true to be true', function() {
   expect(true).toBe(true);
 });
});
```

Now if you run **npm test**, you should see that the test has passed.

Of course, there is much more to testing than this trivial example. Better references can be found in the sample Movies app in the React Native repository.

For instance, here is a shortened version of the test file for getImageSource in the Movies example application (the code is available in its entirety at GitHub (*http://bit.ly/movietestfile*)):

```
jest.dontMock('../getImageSource');
var getImageSource = require('../getImageSource');

describe('getImageSource', () => {
  it('returns null for invalid input', () => {
    expect(getImageSource().uri).toBe(null);
  });
  ...
});
```

Note that you need to explicitly prevent Jest from mocking files, and then require your dependencies afterwards. If you want to read more about Jest, I recommend starting with the documentation (*https://facebook.github.io/jest/*).

When You're Stuck

If you end up with a particularly nasty problem that you can't solve on your own, you can try consulting the community. There are plenty of places to go to ask for advice:

- The #reactnative IRC chat (*irc://chat.freenode.net/reactnative*)
- The React discussion forum (*https://discuss.reactjs.org/*)
- StackOverflow (*http://stackoverflow.com/questions/tagged/react-native*)

If you suspect your issue may be a bug in React Native itself, check the existing list of issues on GitHub (*https://github.com/facebook/react-native/issues*). When reporting issues, it's useful to create a small proof-of-concept application demonstrating the problem.

Summary

In general, debugging with React Native should feel quite similar to debugging your React code on the Web. Most of the tools you'll be familiar with are available here, too, which makes the transition to React Native much easier. That being said, React Native applications bring their own variety of complexity, and sometimes that complexity can manifest in frustrating bugs. Knowing how to debug your applications, and the error messages produced by your environment, will go a long way in helping you to cultivate a productive workflow.

Putting It All Together

Now that we've covered many of the pieces you'll need to build your own React Native applications, let's put everything together. Up until now, we've mostly dealt with small examples. In this chapter, we'll look at the structure of a larger application. We'll cover the use of Reflux, a library for unidirectional dataflow based on the Flux model. We'll also see how we can use the Dimensions API to scale text to accommodate different screen sizes. Finally, we'll end with some homework: tasks that you can undertake to see what it's like to build out more features in an existing React Native codebase.

The Flashcard Application

Zebreto is a flashcard application based on the Spaced Repetition System (SRS), a learning strategy for effective memorization. With SRS, the goal is to review information just before you would otherwise forget it. If you do any foreign language study, you may be familiar with SRS systems; they allow you to memorize large amounts of data more quickly, focusing on long-term retention. A common approach is to start with a small interval between reviews, such as an hour, and to slowly scale up as you get cards correct: first an hour, then a day, then three days, then a week. Intervals can gradually increase to as much as a year, or five years. Tracking these intervals is impractical with pencil-and-paper flashcards, so we'll build an app instead.

Zebreto is a bit more complex than the sample applications we've been building so far. It's meant to model what a more fleshed-out application might look like. All the code is available on GitHub (*https://github.com/bonniee/learning-react-native/tree/master/Zebreto*). It's also entirely cross-platform; the app should work on Android just as it works on iOS.

As illustrated in Figure 9-1, the Zebreto app has three main views:

- The home page, which lists available decks and allows you to create new decks
- The card creation screen
- The review screen

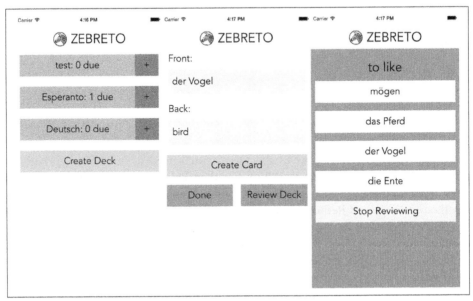

Figure 9-1. Viewing decks, card creation, and card review

Users of the app go through two main interaction flows. The first deals with content creation (i.e., the creation of decks as well as cards). The content creation process works as follows (illustrated in Figure 9-2):

1. The user taps Create Deck.
2. The user enters a deck name, then either taps the Return button or Create Deck again.
3. The user enters values for Front and Back, and then taps Create Card.
4. After entering zero or more cards, the user may tap "Done," bringing them back to the original screen. Alternatively, the user may tap Review Deck and begin reviewing.

Figure 9-2. Creating a deck

Card creation may also be initiated at a later date by tapping the + buttons on the home screen.

The second main interaction flow deals with card review (illustrated in Figure 9-3):

1. The user taps the deck's name that they wish to review.
2. The user is presented with the question screen.
3. The user taps one of the provided options.
4. The user receives feedback based on whether their guess was correct.
5. To view the next review, the user taps Continue.
6. Once all reviews are completed, the user reaches the "Reviews cleared!" screen.

Figure 9-3. Reviewing cards

If the user gets a card correct, we should increase the card's strength, and therefore the interval until it will be seen next. Likewise, for each incorrect card, we'll need to decrease the card's strength, and schedule it for another review soon.

We'll be using the Zebreto app, and in particular the features described above, to talk through some of the patterns and problems that emerge when building a more complete application.

Project Structure

Here's the abbreviated structure of the project:

```
Zebreto
|- .babelrc
|- iOS
|- index.ios.js
|- node_modules
|- package.json
|- src
    |- actions.js
    |- components
    |- data
    |- stores
    |- styles
```

Within the Zebreto folder, our project is loosely split between iOS and Android-specific project folders, and the *src/* directory. The *src/* directory contains all of our React code for the project. Also note that there's a *.babelrc* file, which modifies the default Babel configuration. If you add a *.babelrc* file to the root of a React Native project, the React Native packager will automatically pick it up. In this case, the most significant change is that I've enabled ES6 module syntax:

```
// .babelrc

{
  "stage": 1,
  "optional": ["runtime"],
  "loose": "all",
  "whitelist": [
    "es6.modules"
  ]
}
```

For the most part, we'll be working within the *src/* directory.

Within the *src/* directory, our code is organized further based on functionality:

components/
    All of our React components live here

---

data/
   This is where you'll find our data models

stores/
   Our Reflux data stores, which we'll discuss soon, live here

actions.js
   Reflux actions, which we'll discuss along with the data stores, live here

styles/
   Here you'll find stylesheet objects, which are reused elsewhere

Component Hierarchy

There are three main scenes that may be displayed at any given time. To give you a sense of the general structure of the structure of the application, let's diagram out the component trees for each of the three scenarios.

First, we have deck creation, from the main deck screen. This screen will display as many decks as currently exist in the app, as shown in Figure 9-4. The component hierarchy is diagrammed in Figure 9-5.

Figure 9-4. Creating a deck from the main deck screen

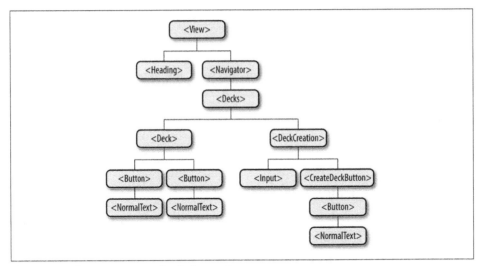

Figure 9-5. Component tree for deck creation

Next, we have the card creation screen (see Figure 9-6).

Figure 9-6. The card creation screen

The component hierarchy for this screen is shown in the diagram in Figure 9-7.

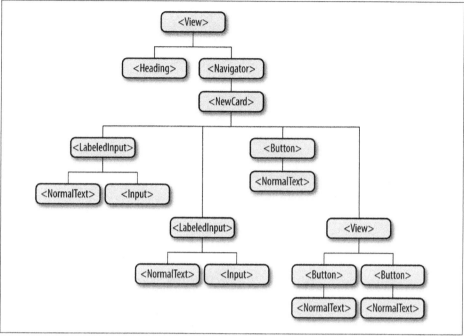

Figure 9-7. Component tree for deck creation

And finally, we have the review screen, which is shown in Figure 9-8. Note that the child component of `<Review>` will change based on where you are in the review flow. After the user has completed all available reviews, `<ViewCard>` will be replaced with information on the user's performance.

Figure 9-8. The card review screen

The component hierarchy for the card review screen is provided in Figure 9-9.

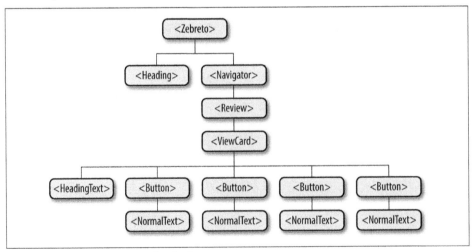

Figure 9-9. Component tree for deck creation

As mentioned earlier, when you're building larger applications it's useful to have some styled components that you can reuse over and over again. As a result, most components don't actually use `<Text>` in order to render text: instead, they use `<Heading Text>` and `<NormalText>`. Similarly, the `<Button>` component is reused frequently. This helps with code readability, and makes creating new components easier.

This should give you a feel for the general structure of the Zebreto application. Note that we still haven't discussed how user interactions are handled, or how we handle the modification and persistence of data. Let's take a look at our data models now.

Modeling and Storing Data

Now that we've seen a bit about how Zebreto handles rendering, how does it handle data? What data do we need to keep track of, and how do we do so?

Zebreto is concerned with two basic models: Cards and Decks.

A Deck consists of a human-readable name and a unique ID. We also sometimes store some metadata about the Cards it contains:

```
Deck: {
  name,
  id,
  totalCards, // computed, may be out of date
  dueCards // computed, may be out of date
}
```

Cards have a front and a back (such as "der Hund" and "the dog"), and belong to a Deck. They also have a strength, represented as an integer, and a due date. Zebreto uses *moment.js* for date objects:

```
Card: {
  front,
  back,
  deckID,
  strength,
  dueDate,
  id
}
```

Decks and Cards could be represented as simple JavaScript objects, but for convenience's sake, Zebreto makes use of some wrapper classes. If you look in the *src/data/* directory, you'll find our model classes. Here's the class for a Deck:

```
// src/data/Deck.js
import md5 from 'md5';

class Deck {
  constructor(name) {
    this.name = name;
```

```
      this.totalCards = 0;
      this.dueCards = 0;
      this.id = md5(name);
   }

   setFromObject(ob) {
      this.name = ob.name;
      this.totalCards = ob.totalCards;
      this.dueCards = ob.dueCards;
      this.id = ob.id;
   }

   resetCounts() {
      this.totalCards = 0;
      this.dueCards = 0;
   }

   static fromObject(ob) {
      let d = new Deck(ob.name);
      d.setFromObject(ob);
      return d;
   }
}

module.exports = Deck;
```

As you can see, the Deck class is quite simple. Its constructor takes in the necessary parameters that distinguish a Deck, and then sets reasonable default values for the other fields. It also provides us with convenience methods for creating a Deck from a JavaScript object, and an easy way to reset the metadata stored on the Deck.

For now, the so-called unique IDs are constructed by taking the MD5 hash of relevant info.

The Card class looks fairly similar, and provides us with helper methods to create a Card from an ordinary object:

```
// src/data/Card.js

import md5 from 'md5';
import moment from 'moment';

class Card {
   constructor(front, back, deckID) {
      this.front = front;
      this.back = back;
      this.deckID = deckID;
      this.strength = 0;
      this.dueDate = moment();
      this.id = md5(front + back + deckID);
   }
```

```
  setFromObject(ob) {
    this.front = ob.front;
    this.back = ob.back;
    this.deckID = ob.deckID;
    this.strength = ob.strength;
    this.dueDate = moment(ob.dueDate);
    this.id = ob.id;
  }

  static fromObject(ob) {
    let c = new Card(ob.front, ob.back, ob.deckID);
    c.setFromObject(ob);
    return c;
  }
}

module.exports = Card;
```

To understand how these models are used in the application, let's look at our data flow architecture.

Data Flow Architecture: Reflux and Flux

Zebreto uses Reflux for its data flow architecture, which is based on the Flux pattern. Previous examples we've looked at in this book haven't required much in the way of data flow management. With smaller applications, communicating between components is usually a trivial issue. Consider the case where a button tap has an impact on the parent's state:

```
// Child.js
import React from 'react-native';
var {Text, TouchableOpacity} = React;

export default React.createClass({
  render() {
    <TouchableOpacity onPress={this.props.onPress}>
      <Text>Child Component</Text>
    </TouchableOpacity>
  }
});
```

By passing a callback from the parent to the child, the parent can be alerted about interactions with the child:

```
// Parent.js
import React from 'react-native';
import Child from './Child';

export default React.createClass({
  getInitialState() {
    return {
      numTaps: 0
```

```
    }
  },
  _handlePress() {
    this.setState({numTaps: this.state.numTaps + 1});
  },
  render() {
    <Child onPress={this._handlePress}/>
  }
});
```

For simple use cases, this pattern works just fine.

Our need for a more robust data flow architecture becomes apparent when we consider a more complex interaction. What happens when a component much farther down the component tree needs to impact an application state located on a higher level? Let's look at the review screen again (Figure 9-10).

Figure 9-10. Reviewing cards

When you select one of the answers, the following things need to happen:

1. The app provides visual feedback indicating if you were correct or not
2. The next review is made available
3. The card's strength value is updated, if appropriate
4. The number of available reviews for the deck is updated, if appropriate

If you were to quit the Zebreto application midway through a review, you'd want your information to be saved, so all of these changes to state *should* happen each time you select a review. Let's take a look at the component tree again (Figure 9-11):

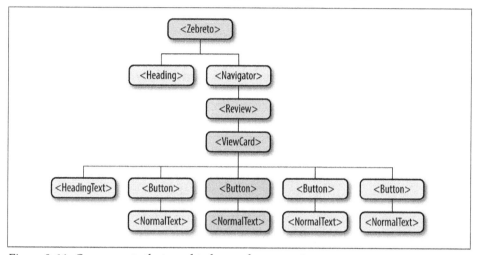

Figure 9-11. Components that need to know about a review

The top-level Zebreto component needs to receive this update, as do the `<Review>` and `<ViewCard>` components. Passing callbacks around doesn't scale very well to this use case, so we'll use a Flux-like data architecture instead.

Flux is more of a pattern than a formal framework. The key concept is unidirectional data flow. In React, props and state are passed from parent to child; this unidirectional flow means that rendering is performant, and our application state is easier to think about.

Passing lots of callbacks around breaks that flow, and can essentially result in two-way data binding, where cascading updates can be triggered in unpredictable ways. By using a Flux-like application architecture (illustrated in Figure 9-12), we can separate out changes in application state from the pieces of UI that can trigger them, and maintain the unidirectional pattern.

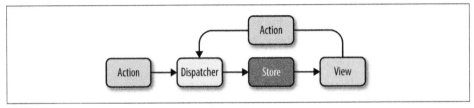

Figure 9-12. Data propagation in the Flux architecture

With the Flux pattern, views render based on information that they get from their stores. Actions can be triggered by user interactions with a view, or by other events, such as app initializiation. The dispatcher handles incoming actions and passes them along to stores.

Flux is the official Facebook archiecture for this problem, but others in the React community have built Flux-inspired libraries that seek to solve many of the same problems. Reflux, illustrated in Figure 9-13, is a particularly popular one, and we'll use it for Zebreto.

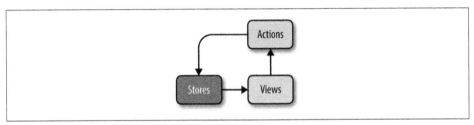

Figure 9-13. Data propagation in the Reflux architecture

With Reflux, you don't have a concept of a dispatcher. There are simply views, stores, and actions, and stores can listen to actions directly.

Adding Reflux to a React Native project is as easy as npm install:

```
npm install --save reflux
```

Using Reflux in Zebreto

Let's look at how Reflux is used in our application.

In Zebreto, we have multiple stores (illustrated in Figure 9-14):

DeckMetaStore
    Contains Deck metadata, such as the number of pending reviews

CardsStore
    Contains all Cards

```
ReviewStore
```
   Contains the reviews for the current Deck

Stores can listen to each other. In Zebreto, reviews are constructed based on informa-tion obtained from both `CardsStore` and `DeckMetaStore`, so the `ReviewStore` listens to both of them. This relationship is shown in Figure 9-14.

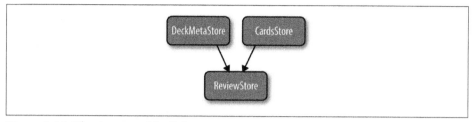

Figure 9-14. The stores used in Zebreto

We also have multiple actions, defined in our *actions.js* file:

```
// src/actions.js

import Reflux from 'reflux';

export var DeckActions = Reflux.createActions([
  'createDeck',
  'deleteDeck',
  'reviewDeck',
  'deleteAllDecks'
]);

export var CardActions = Reflux.createActions([
  'createCard',
  'deleteCard',
  'review',
  'editCard',
  'deleteAllCards'
]);
```

Any component can trigger an action that stores can listen to, which may then cause cascading effects.

To return to our example of reviewing a card, the Reflux data flow pattern works as follows:

- The user selects an answer, which triggers the `CardActions.review` action.
- The `ReviewStore` listens for `CardActions.review` actions, and processes the new information.
- If appropriate, the `ReviewStore` triggers a `CardActions.editCard` action.

- The `CardsStore` listens to `CardActions.editCard` actions. It will persist the relevant change to `AsyncStorage` and then trigger an update.

- The top-level `<Zebreto>` component listens for updates to the `CardsStore`, and updates its `state` accordingly.

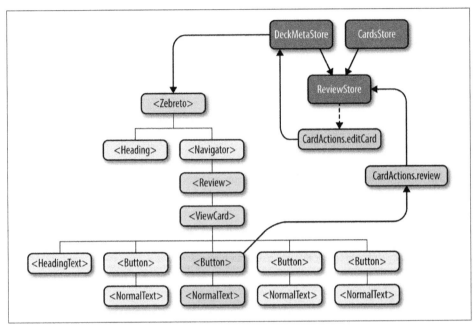

Figure 9-15. Handling updates after a card review

As another example, deck creation works as follows:

- The create deck button fires a `DeckActions.createDeck` action.

- The create deck button also invokes a callback prop to cause the Navigator to transition scenes to the card creation screen.

- The `DeckMetaStore` is listening to `DeckActions.createDeck`; it creates a new Deck and persists it to `AsyncStorage`.

Persistence, AsyncStorage, and the Reflux Stores

Zebreto persists user data to `AsyncStorage` through simple JSON serialization. This is handled via the stores, as the stores are the central source of truth regarding application state. For example, let's look at the `CardsStore`:

```
// src/stores/CardsStore.js

import Card from './../data/Card';
import Reflux from 'reflux';
import _ from 'lodash';
import {CardActions} from './../actions';

import React from 'react-native';
var { AsyncStorage } = React;

const CARD_KEY = 'zebreto-cards';

var cardsStore = Reflux.createStore({
  init() {
    this._loadCards().done();
    this.listenTo(CardActions.createCard, this.createCard);
    this.listenTo(CardActions.deleteAllCards, this.deleteAllCards);
    this.listenTo(CardActions.editCard, this.editCard);
    this._cards = [];
    this.emit();
  },

  async _loadCards() {
    try {
      var val = await AsyncStorage.getItem(CARD_KEY);
      if (val !== null) {
        this._cards = JSON.parse(val).map((cardObj) => {
          return Card.fromObject(cardObj);
        });
        this.emit();
      }
      else {
        console.info(`${CARD_KEY} not found on disk.`);
      }
    }
    catch (error) {
      console.error('AsyncStorage error: ', error.message);
    }
  },

  async _writeCards() {
    try {
      await AsyncStorage.setItem(CARD_KEY, JSON.stringify(this._cards));
    }
    catch (error) {
      console.error('AsyncStorage error: ', error.message);
    }
  },

  deleteAllCards() {
    this._cards = [];
    this.emit();
```

```
    },

    editCard(newCard) {
      // Assume newCard.id corresponds to an existing card.
      let match = _.find(this._cards, (card) => {
        return card.id === newCard.id;
      });
      match.setFromObject(newCard);
      this.emit();

    },

    createCard(front, back, deckID) {
      this._cards.push(new Card(front, back, deckID));
      this.emit();
    },

    emit() {
      this._writeCards().done();
      this.trigger(this._cards);
    }
  });

  export default cardsStore;
```

The `CardsStore` is the only point in the Zebreto app that handles reading and writing data relating to cards. For now, this is done via calls to `AsyncStorage` in the `_load Cards()` and `_writeCards()` functions. If we wanted to update how we store cards—for instance, to use a SQLite database instead, or to fetch data via a network call—we could easily do so by updating these two methods.

Also worth noting is that the `CardsStore` loads stored data when it is initialized, in its `init()` method; and persists cards to `AsyncStorage` whenever they are updated, in the `emit()` method. Thus, even when the user quits the application, their data will be saved.

Using the Navigator

Another point of possible interest is the use of the `<Navigator>` component in Zebreto. Let's look at the source code for the root component:

```
// src/components/Zebreto.js
import React from 'react-native';
var {
  StyleSheet,
  View,
  Navigator
} = React;

import Reflux from 'reflux';
```

```javascript
import {DeckActions} from './../actions';

import Decks from './Decks';
import Review from './Review';
import NewCard from './NewCard';
import Heading from './Header';

import CardsStore from './../stores/CardsStore';
import DeckMetaStore from './../stores/DeckMetaStore';

var Zebreto = React.createClass({
  displayName: 'Zebreto',

  mixins: [Reflux.connect(DeckMetaStore, 'deckMetas')],

  componentWillMount() {
    CardsStore.emit();
  },

  review(deckID) {
    DeckActions.reviewDeck(deckID);
    this.refs.navigator.push({
      name: 'review',
      data: {
        deckID: deckID
      }
    });
  },

  createdDeck(deck) {
    this.refs.navigator.push({
      name: 'createCards',
      data: {
        deck: deck
      }
    });
  },

  goHome() {
    this.refs.navigator.popToTop();
  },

  _renderScene(route) { ❷
    switch (route.name) {
    case 'decks':
      return <Decks review={this.review}
        createdDeck={this.createdDeck}/>;
    case 'createCards':
      return <NewCard
        review={this.review}
        quit={this.goHome}
        nextCard={this.createdDeck}
```

```
         {...route.data}/>;
      case 'review':  ❸
        return <Review quit={this.goHome} {...route.data} />;
      default:
        console.error('Encountered unexpected route: ' + route.name);
      }
      return <Decks/>;
    },

    render() {  ❶
      return (
        <View style={styles.container}>
          <Heading/>
          <Navigator
            ref='navigator'
            initialRoute=
            renderScene={this._renderScene}/>
        </View>
      );
    }
});

var styles = StyleSheet.create({
  container: {
    flex: 1,
    marginTop: 30
  }
});

export default Zebreto;
```

There's a fair bit going on in this file, so we'll take it in chunks:

❶   The render method is actually quite small. We wrap everything in a `<View>`, then render the header, which contains the logo; and the `<Navigator>`, which renders the appropriate scene. As we can see from the `_renderScene()` method, and as discussed earlier, there are three possible scenes: `decks`, `createCards`, and `review`. Thus, at the top level, the app consists of one wrapper component, with two children.

❷   `_renderScene()` also takes care of attaching the appropriate data and callbacks to each scene, as props. It uses spread syntax to do so more effectively. If you haven't seen spread syntax often before, it's a nice feature, taken from ES6. As an example, if we invoked `_renderScene()` as follows, it will return the code listed in the next callout.

```
_renderScene({
  data: {
    someProp: 'whatever',
```

```
    anotherProp: 2
  }
});
```

❸ By using spread syntax, _renderScene() would return the equivalent to the following:

```
return (
  <Review
    quit={this.goHome}
    someProp="whatever"
    anotherProp={2} />);
```

So, there's our root <Zebreto> component. It holds a ref to the <Navigator> component, and manages the various scenes. For the most part, however, the more complex functionality is left to the individual scenes.

By placing the <Navigator> and the _renderScene() logic in the top-level component, and passing in callbacks such as goHome() as props to the individual scenes, the scenes themselves do not need to be aware of the navigational structure. Instead, we keep all of the navigation-related rendering logic in the <Zebreto> component.

If we wanted to replace the <Navigator> with something platform specific (e.g., a <NavigatorIOS> component), it would be easy to do so, because its usage is limited to just this file. (We would just need to create a *Zebreto.ios.js* and *Zebreto.android.js* file, respectively.) Even though we don't need to right now, it's nice to have the navigation visible and isolated within the top-level component.

A Look at Third-Party Dependencies

We should also examine the outside libraries used in the application. Zebreto doesn't have *too* many third-party dependencies, but it does have some. Take a look at *package.json*:

```
// package.json

{
  "name": "Zebreto",
  "version": "0.0.1",
  "private": true,
  "scripts": {
    "start": "node_modules/react-native/packager/packager.sh"
  },
  "dependencies": {
    "lodash": "^3.10.1",
    "md5": "^2.0.0",
    "moment": "^2.10.6",
    "react": "^0.13.3",
    "react-native": "^0.11.2",
```

```
      "reflux": "^0.2.12"
    }
  }
```

react-native and react are obvious dependencies. We've covered reflux, too. moment is used for date objects, and md5 is used for calculating card and deck IDs. Finally, lodash gives us some nice utility functions, and we use it for shuffling card reviews.

It's worth noting that none of these libraries were built with React Native or mobile in mind, and they work as is without any tinkering necessary. Huzzah!

Responsive Design and Font Sizes

In order for your application to support multiple devices properly, your UI will need to accommodate some variation in screen size. To some degree, flexbox-based styles handle this for you without any special attention.

Font styles, however, often require explicit adjustments based on screen size. The reusable text components in Zebreto scale the font size based on screen width in order to accommodate different device sizes (Figure 9-16).

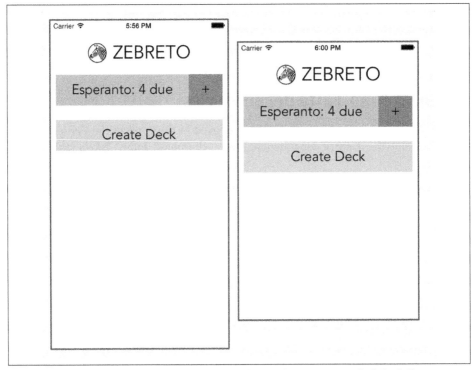

Figure 9-16. The font size on an iPhone 4S and an iPhone 6 is just slightly different

Handling different font sizes is pretty easy. Let's look at how font scaling is handled in Zebreto.

In the *styles/* directory, we export the font-related stylesheets from *fonts.js*, as well as scaling factors to use later:

```
// src/styles/fonts.js
import { StyleSheet } from 'react-native';

var fonts = StyleSheet.create({
  normal: {
    fontSize: 24,
    fontFamily: 'Avenir Medium'
  },

  alternate: {
    fontSize: 50,
    fontFamily: 'Avenir Heavy',
    color: '#FFFFFF'
  },

  big: {
    fontSize: 32,
    alignSelf: 'center',
    fontFamily: 'Avenir Medium'
  }
});

var scalingFactors = {
  normal: 15,
  big: 7
};

module.exports = {fonts, scalingFactors};
```

Then, in our text components, such as <NormalText>, we get the screen dimensions. The Dimensions API is available as a polyfill once we require it:

```
import Dimensions from 'Dimensions';
let {width, height} = Dimensions.get('window');
```

Now we have the screen dimensions to work with, available as the variables width and height.

For <NormalText>, we use just the width value, in conjunction with our scaling factor, to determine the font size:

```
var scaled = StyleSheet.create({
  normal: {
    fontSize: width / scalingFactors.normal
  }
});
```

We then use this stylesheet in our component:

```
// src/components/NormalText.js

import React from 'react-native';
var {
  StyleSheet,
  Text,
  View
} = React;

import {fonts, scalingFactors} from './../styles/fonts';
import Dimensions from 'Dimensions';
let {width} = Dimensions.get('window');

var NormalText = React.createClass({
  displayName: 'NormalText',

  propTypes: {
    style: View.propTypes.style
  },

  render() {
    return (
      <Text style={[this.props.style, fonts.normal, scaled.normal]}>
        {this.props.children}
      </Text>
      );
  }
});

var scaled = StyleSheet.create({
  normal: {
    fontSize: width / scalingFactors.normal
  }
});

export default NormalText;
```

And that's it! The <HeadingText> component takes the same approach, so whenever we use <HeadingText> or <NormalText> elsewhere in the application, the font size should be scaled appropriately.

Summary and Homework

The Zebreto application is meant to serve as a reference. In many ways, it's a "minimum viable project," and there are plenty of ways it could be improved. That being said, there's still plenty to explore in the codebase, and I encourage you to dig into it.

If you want to get some more practice working within the context of React Native, I encourage you to check out the GitHub repository and try extending Zebreto. Here are some ideas to get you started:

- Add the ability to delete decks
- Add a screen where you can view all cards in a deck
- Display statistics about the card strengths in a deck
- Experiment with different styles
- Change the Decks component to use a ListView

In the next chapter, we'll walk through the process of actually shipping Zebreto—or your own application!—to the App Store.

Deploying to the iOS App Store

Now that you have a *totally awesome* application, you'll want to get it into the hands of your users. This process will vary by platform. In this chapter, we will focus on the detailed steps for uploading an application to the iOS App Store.

As web developers, we're used to having more control over our deploy processes. You may be accustomed to shipping code to production many times in a single day, and versions are usually a nonissue. With the iOS App Store, deployment is significantly more complicated, and new version releases usually require 1–2 weeks of review. Thus, it's important to take the App Store submission and review process into account during your planning phase.

Preparing Your Xcode Project

Your Xcode project contains a lot of metadata about your application. React Native sets up some values for you by default, but before we submit our application for review, we'll need to ensure that certain attributes are set properly. In the case of Zebreto, our project file is located in *iOS/Zebreto.xcodeproj*.

If, for some reason, you haven't done so already, make sure that your Xcode project file is checked into version control. It's not unheard of for Xcode to crash while attempting to edit a project, leaving your project file in a bad state.

Open your project in Xcode (Figure 10-1). You'll want to open the left pane, and close the right and bottom panes (the controls for this are in the top-right corner).

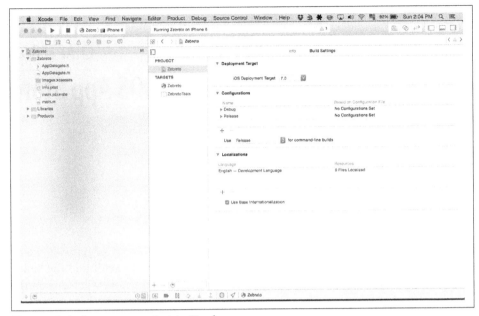

Figure 10-1. Open your project in Xcode

Selecting Supported Devices and Target iOS Version

You'll need to decide which version of iOS your project should target. Confusingly, there are two separate, but related, settings for this: the Base SDK version, and the iOS deployment target. By default, React Native sets the deployment target to 7.0, and uses the latest iOS SDK (9.0). The deployment target is the minimum iOS version required to run your application, while the SDK version determines which SDK version your application will be built against. The difference in these values is documented by Apple (*http://apple.co/1MVKVc3*).

For our purposes, just remember that the Base SDK version needs to be greater than or equal to the iOS deployment target.

If you are using any iOS APIs that require a higher version than specified by default, you will need to change the deployment target value appropriately. You can change this under the Info menu for your project (Figure 10-2).

Figure 10-2. Selecting your target iOS version

If you want to update the Base SDK version, it's specified under the Build Settings menu (Figure 10-3).

Figure 10-3. Changing the Base SDK version

If you select your application (under TARGETS) instead of your project, you can also choose which devices and screen orientations your application supports. Namely, for iOS projects, you can designate your application as iPhone-only, iPad-only, or Universal, meaning that it supports both iPad and iPhone (Figure 10-4).

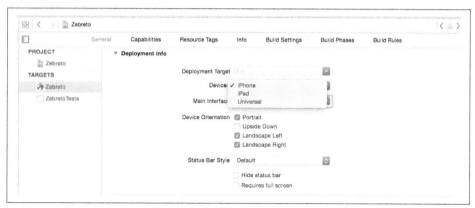

Figure 10-4. Setting the device targets

Once you've checked which devices you want to support, we can move on to setting the launch image and application icons.

Launch Screen Images

The launch screen image is the placeholder image that appears when the user launches your application, while the app is loading. There are multiple appropriate approaches here. Some applications choose to use a "splash screen," with their application's logo and name. Other applications opt for a screen that mimics the app's user interface, but without any data filled in, so that the transition appears more seamless.

Regardless of which approach you take, you'll need to provide your launch screen image in sizes appropriate for all devices you support.

Begin by selecting your project's *Image.xcassets/* directory, and creating a new launch image set (Figure 10-5).

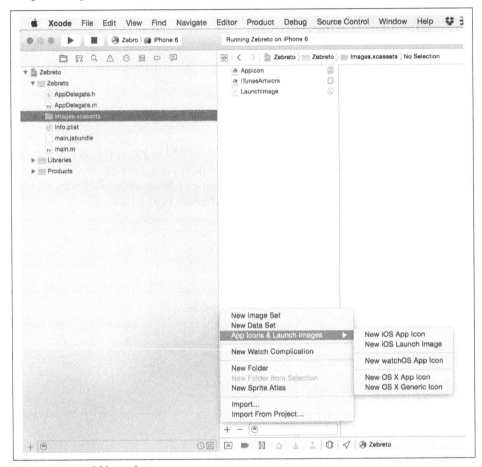

Figure 10-5. Add launch images

From here, you'll be given the opportunity to add appropriately sized launch images for every relevant device size (Figure 10-6). Phew! That's a lot.

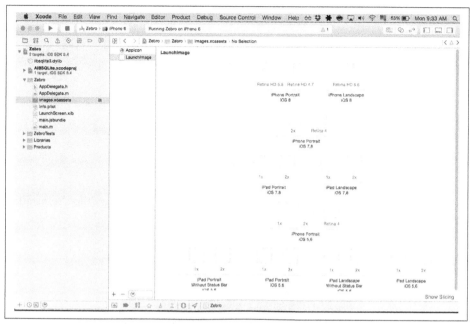

Figure 10-6. Adding launch images for each device size and orientation

The required dimensions vary by device. For instance, the iPhone 6 requires a 750 x 1334px file for portrait mode, and a 1334 x 750px file for landscape mode.

For specific required dimensions, consult Apple's documentation (*http://apple.co/ 1HaVNmb*). Xcode will generate warnings if you provide an incorrectly sized file, so you can also use that to guide you.

Adding Your Application Icon

You application icon is what appears on the user's home screen, as well as within the App Store. Like the launch screen, you should provide application icon assets in sizes appropriate to your application's supported devices, and check your sizes against Apple's documentation (*http://apple.co/1HaVNmb*).

Apple's Human Interface Guidelines set out some basic guidelines. Application icons should not contain any transparent areas, and should be square. (Apple applies the rounded-corners effect to your icons; you need not do this yourself.)

Click the plus button while your *Image.xcassets/* folder is selected, just as you did earlier for the Launch Image. This time, however, create a new App Icon instead (Figure 10-7).

Figure 10-7. Add icons to your project

You can drag and drop files here in order to add them as icons.

If you delete your application from the simulator or your device and then reinstall it, you should now see your icon, just like in Figure 10-8.

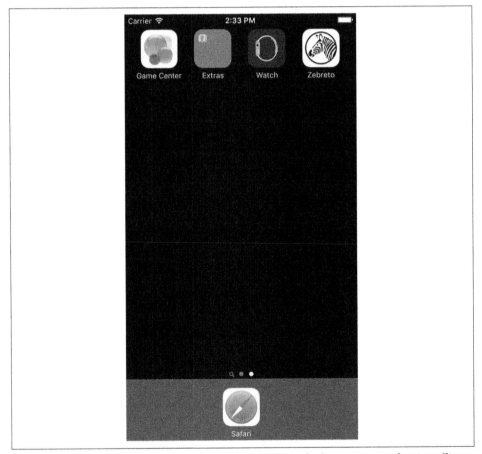

Figure 10-8. After setting a custom icon, you'll see it on the home screen after installing your app, even during development

If, for some reason, your Launch Image or your App Icon isn't rendering properly, be sure to check the values under App Icons and Launch Images, which you'll find in the General settings menu.

Figure 10-9. Double-check the App Icons Source and Launch Images Source files

Setting Your Bundle Name

The bundle name of your project in Xcode determines what your application will be named on the user's device, so it's very important.

Note that Xcode sometimes chokes when it attempts to rename files, and can actually corrupt your project file. Ensure that your project file is checked into a version control system before attempting to use Xcode's renaming functionality.

We can view and edit this value under the Identity and Type section in the right-hand menu pane (Figure 10-10). This value is set for you when you run `react-native init`, but if you want to change the name, now's the time to do so.

Figure 10-10. The Name under the Identity and Type menu is user-facing

Updating AppDelegate.m

Recall how in *AppDelegate.m*, there are two ways to specify the JavaScript code location: from a bundled file, or from localhost. Running the React Native packager in development is fine, but for deployment we'll want to generate a bundled JavaScript file.

Comment out the first option, which uses localhost, and enable the second option, which loads from the bundled file:

```
// jsCodeLocation =
// [NSURL URLWithString:@"http://localhost:8081/index.ios.bundle"];

    ...

jsCodeLocation = [[NSBundle mainBundle]
URLForResource:@"main" withExtension:@"jsbundle"];
```

Having done this, we'll need to generate the bundle.

From your project directory, run:

```
react-native bundle --minify
```

It's a good idea to confirm that your application still works in the simulator after this. Restart the simulator and try launching your application. It ought to work as usual.

Set Schema for Release

Next, we need to set the build scheme for Release, instead of Debug. As shown in Figure 10-11, navigate to Product → Scheme → Edit Scheme....

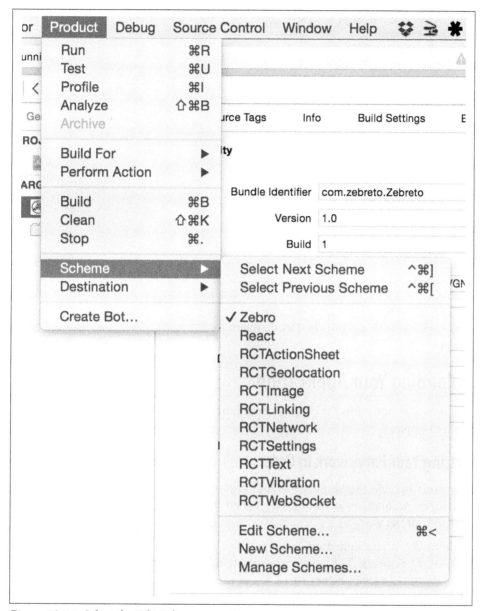

Figure 10-11. Select the Edit Scheme… option

Then change your project scheme to Release (Figure 10-12).

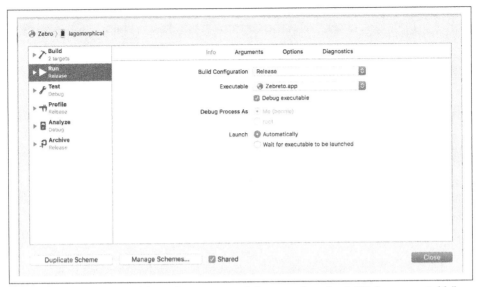

Figure 10-12. Set the Build Configuration to Release and uncheck "Debug executable"

This means that things like the Debug menu won't appear when you run your application.

Uploading Your Application

OK, now that our project is properly configured for release, it's time to actually submit it to Apple!

Getting Your Paperwork in Order

You won't be able to submit your application to the App Store without an Apple Developer Account, so if you haven't signed up yet, now's the time! It will set you back $99 for the year.

Additionally, if you signed up previously, you may find that you need to sign some updated agreements. The error messages that indicate this are not always easy to parse, as you can see in Figure 10-13.

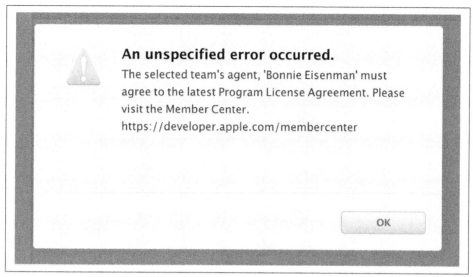

Figure 10-13. If you see this kind of error, first attempt to follow the instructions provided

Unfortunately, visiting the specified URL (*https://developer.apple.com/membercenter*) sometimes produces a similar error, as shown in Figure 10-14.

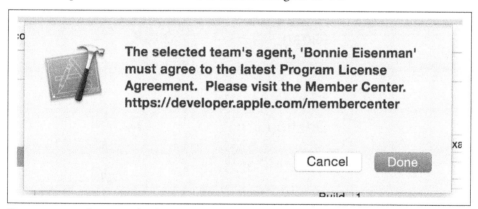

Figure 10-14. If you see this kind of error, visit iTunes Connect and check for any outstanding paperwork

If you run into these kinds of issues, head first to iTunes Connect (*https://itunescon nect.apple.com*), *not* the Member Center. From there, select Agreements, Tax, and Banking, and fill out any remaining forms.

Creating an Archive

The next step is to create an Archive of your application to submit to the App Store. This action is located in the menu under Product → Archive.

If Archive is grayed out (as in Figure 10-15), it's probably because you have the iOS Simulator selected as your build target.

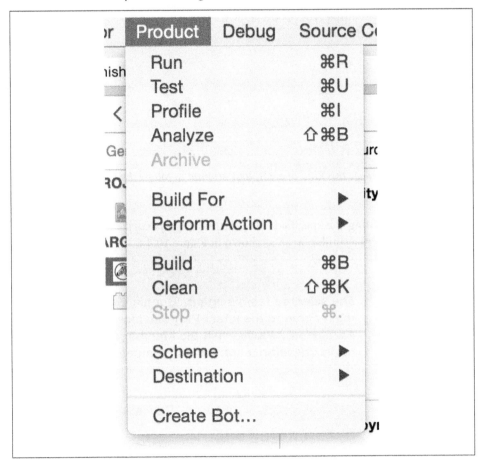

Figure 10-15. If the Archive option is disabled, try changing your build target

Change your build target to be an iOS device, and you should be able to select Archive from the menu.

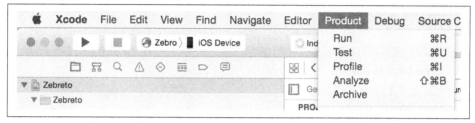

Figure 10-16. Select Product → Archive to begin the archive creation process

If successful, the Archives screen will appear (Figure 10-17).

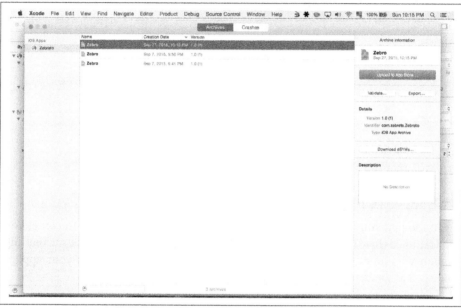

Figure 10-17. Choose an archive to upload to the App Store

Ready to hit that Upload to the App Store button? Go for it! Xcode will run a few last checks, and then you'll be able to send your application to Apple (Figure 10-18).

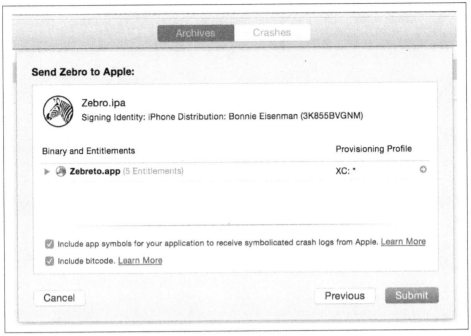

Figure 10-18. Press Submit to send your archive to the App Store

Creating an App in iTunes Connect

If you thought you were done at this point, I'm sorry, there's still more to come! Your application archive has been uploaded, but now you need to prepare your actual submission via iTunes Connect. This includes important metadata about your application, such as the description and screenshots, which will be user-facing.

For more in-depth information about this process, you can consult Apple's documentation (*http://apple.co/1S6zsXq*) about creating an iTunes Connect record.

First, you'll need to register an App ID in the Developer Center (*http://apple.co/1NLquel*). The form will require you to enter a Bundle Identifier for your application (Figure 10-19).

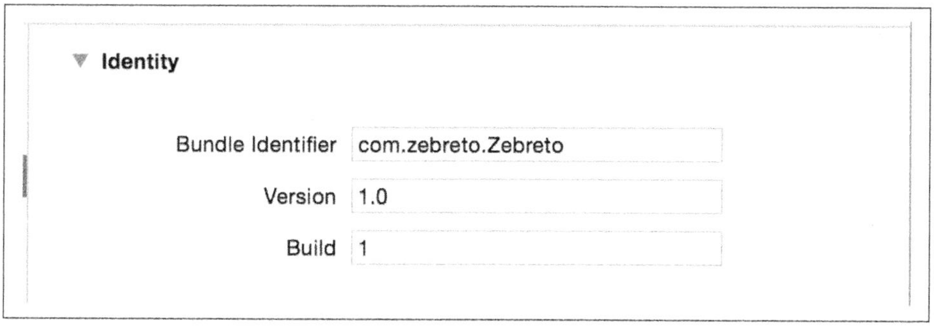

Identity

Bundle Identifier	com.zebreto.Zebreto
Version	1.0
Build	1

Figure 10-19. Setting the Bundle Identifier in Xcode

This should match the Bundle Identifier listed in your Xcode project (located under the Identity menu); see Figure 10-20.

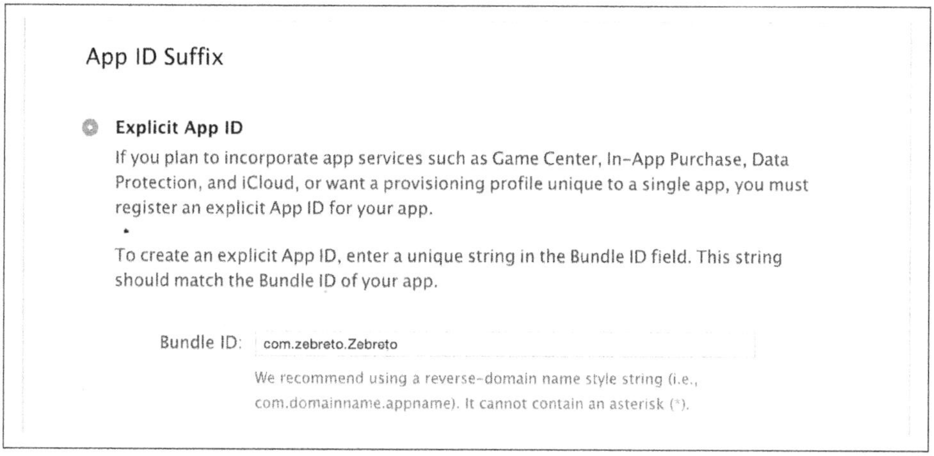

App ID Suffix

○ **Explicit App ID**
   If you plan to incorporate app services such as Game Center, In–App Purchase, Data
   Protection, and iCloud, or want a provisioning profile unique to a single app, you must
   register an explicit App ID for your app.
   •
   To create an explicit App ID, enter a unique string in the Bundle ID field. This string
   should match the Bundle ID of your app.

   Bundle ID: com.zebreto.Zebreto

   We recommend using a reverse-domain name style string (i.e.,
   com.domainname.appname). It cannot contain an asterisk (*).

Figure 10-20. The Bundle ID in the Developer Center should match the Bundle Identifier from Xcode

Bundle Identifiers

If your Bundle Identifiers don't match, you won't be able to associate your application archive with its iTunes Connect record. Be sure to double-check!

Next, we can create a new application in iTunes Connect (*https://itunescon nect.apple.com*) (Figure 10-21).

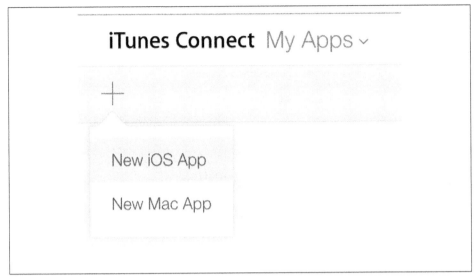

Figure 10-21. Select New iOS App to create a new app from iTunes Connect

Once again, the Bundle Identifier appears. Select the appropriate one and go on to create your application.

If your application archive upload was successful, you'll see your build appear in iTunes Connect (Figure 10-22).

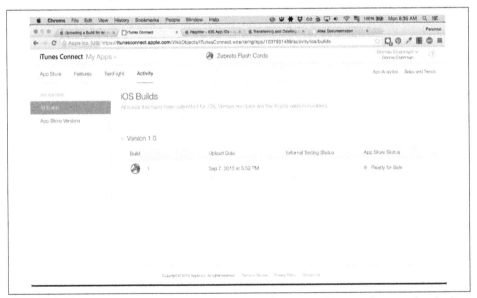

Figure 10-22. After uploading your application archive, it will appear here under the list of builds

If you don't see any builds here, try checking the following:

- Do the Bundle IDs in your iTunes Connect record and Xcode project match?
- Did Xcode produce any errors when you attempted to upload the archive?
- What happens when you reupload your application archive?

From iTunes Connect, you'll now be able to enter information related to your application's App Store listing (e.g., the correct categorization, description, etc.). There's plenty of information to fill out, so take your time.

One important field of note: this page also lets you upload screenshots and video walkthroughs of your application. Providing good-quality screenshots is critical to your application's success in the App Store. As usual, you'll need to provide appropriately sized screenshots for each type of supported device (Figure 10-23).

Figure 10-23. Uploading screenshots

Screenshots and the iOS Simulator

You can use the iOS simulator to easily obtain appropriately sized screenshots. Load each device type and hit Command+S to save a screenshot.

Beta Testing with TestFlight

Before you submit your application for review in the App Store, you should use Test-Flight for beta testing. Even if you're the only "beta tester," working with TestFlight rather than a development-mode application gives you a more accurate experience of what your application will be like once downloaded freshly onto a user's device.

TestFlight allows you to easily send email invitations for testing to users. Under your application's record in iTunes Connect, select TestFlight, and add your beta testers (Figure 10-24). You'll need their email addresses in order to do so.

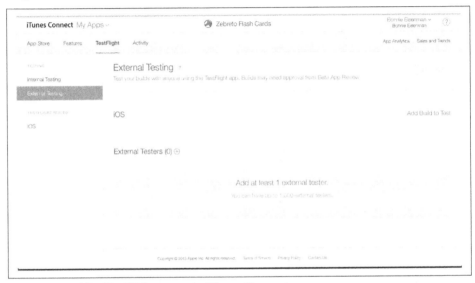

Figure 10-24. The TestFlight screen in iTunes Connect

Your beta testers will first need to install the TestFlight app. Then, once they receive the email invitation to test your application, TestFlight will give them the option of installing your application (Figure 10-25). Once installed, the application will behave like any other.

Figure 10-25. Beta testers will receive an email invitation via TestFlight, which will allow them to install the app

Submitting the Application for Review

After you're satisfied with your beta testers' feedback, and you've filled out all of the relevant information in iTunes Connect, you can (finally!) submit your application for review. After submission, iTunes Connect will note that your application's status is "Waiting for Review" (Figure 10-26).

Figure 10-26. Your application status is viewable in iTunes Connect

You will receive email updates once your application makes it to the front of the review queue, and once it is rejected or accepted. On average, the App Store review process seems to take 1–2 weeks, and there's no easy way to tell how far along your application is. Review times will lengthen during the busiest times of year, such as the holiday season.

To give you a point of reference, Zebreto was accepted after an eight-day wait. After your application is accepted, congrats; it should now be available for download in the App Store.

Summary

After putting in the hard work to create your application, releasing it to your users can feel exhilarating! However, releasing your application is just the beginning, as you'll have to support your application postrelease. Unlike the Web, where you can deploy often and easily, new iOS versions take time, and have a longer lifespan. Many iOS users don't have auto-updating enabled, so every version counts. And at minimum you'll need to wait for Apple to review your application each time you wish to submit an update or a bugfix. (For truly critical bugfixes, you can request an expedited review, but use these carefully!)

Furthermore, iOS releases are somewhat risky in terms of your application's rating. Your average review, displayed on the app's page in the App Store, is based on the current version, not its overall rating, so a buggy release can really hurt you. Remember, testing is your friend!

When you have a new version of your application to submit, the process is very similar to the initial upload process. Bump your application version in Xcode, then submit a new archive. You'll find options to submit a new build for review in iTunes Connect.

Now that we've covered how to submit your application to the iOS App Store, in the next chapter we'll turn our attention to how the analogous process works for Android.

Deploying Android Applications

All right! You've made it this far; ready to deploy your Android app and get it into your users' hands? If you've already gone through the iOS app submission process, plenty here will feel familiar, though happily the Play Store approval process is simpler. Review is faster, too: you can expect it to take 1–2 business days for your application to be approved.

In this chapter, we'll cover what you'll need to do to generate a deploy-ready APK of your React Native application, how to distribute it to your beta testers, and how to submit it to the Google Play Store for review.

Check the Docs!

We'll be doing a detailed walkthrough of how to deploy your Android application here, but you'll always want to consult the official documentation (*https://facebook.github.io/react-native/docs/signed-apk-android.html*) for the most up-to-date procedures.

Setting Application Icon

While the default Android icon is kinda cute, you'll want to replace it with a custom application icon before you deploy your application.

The application icon is specified in *android/app/src/main/AndroidManifest.xml*:

```
android:icon="@mipmap/ic_launcher"
```

That filepath refers to a path within *android/app/src/main/res/*. You may recall from Chapter 3 that Android image resources are located in different folders based on their resolution. The icon file is no different. You'll notice that the default icon is already present in your application (Figure 11-1).

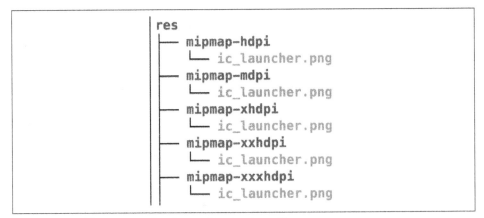

Figure 11-1. File structure for the application icon files

You can just replace these files directly, or change the icon path in your *AndroidManifest.xml* to point to a different location. When you reinstall your application onto the device, you'll see that it's using your new icon (Figure 11-2).

Figure 11-2. Viewing our installed apps, now with a custom icon for Zebreto

If creating app icons in the various resolutions sounds tedious, try using a tool that generates the appropriate sizes for you. I am personally a fan of romannurik's project (*https://romannurik.github.io/AndroidAssetStudio/icons-launcher.html*).

Building the APK for Release

To deploy an Android application, we need to generate a release APK (an APK is an Android application package file, the format used to distribute Android applications). There are five basic steps here:

1. Generate a signing key.
2. Set up gradle variables.
3. Add signing config to application's gradle config.
4. Generate the release APK.
5. Install release APK on a device.

We'll walk through them one by one. You may also want to read Android's official Publishing Overview (*http://bit.ly/21cvRNw*) for more context.

First, you'll need to generate a signing key for your application.

You can use `keytool` to generate a keystore and key:

```
$ keytool -genkey -v -keystore my-release-key.keystore \
    -alias my-key-alias -keyalg RSA -keysize 2048 -validity 10000
```

The Android docs (*http://developer.android.com/tools/publishing/app-signing.html*) have more information about application signing. Android uses certificate signing to identify the author of an application. Don't forget your passphrase, and don't lose your key. You'll need these to release updates to your application!

The preceding command will generate a *my-release-key.keystore* file. Move it into the *android/app/* directory in your project.

Then, create or edit the file *~/.gradle/gradle.properties* and add the code provided in Example 11-1.

Example 11-1. Add these variables to ~/.gradle/gradle.properties

```
MYAPP_RELEASE_STORE_FILE=my-release-key.keystore
MYAPP_RELEASE_KEY_ALIAS=my-key-alias
MYAPP_RELEASE_STORE_PASSWORD=*****
MYAPP_RELEASE_KEY_PASSWORD=*****
```

Replace the asterisks with the password you used when invoking `keytool` earlier.

By placing these in our ~/.gradle/gradle.properties file, we're including them in our general gradle configuration. (Remember, gradle is the build system used for our React Native projects.)

Be Careful with Your Keys!

Don't check your key passwords into version control! And don't lose your keys. After publishing your application, if you want to use a new key, you'll need to create a fresh Play Store entry, and you'll lose all of your download stats and reviews.

Now that we've set up our gradle variables, we need to add our signing config to our application's gradle config. Open up the *android/app/build.gradle* file and add the signing config (Example 11-2).

Example 11-2. Modifications to android/app/build.gradle

```
...
android {
  ...
  defaultConfig { ... }
  signingConfigs {
    release {
      storeFile file(MYAPP_RELEASE_STORE_FILE)
      storePassword MYAPP_RELEASE_STORE_PASSWORD
      keyAlias MYAPP_RELEASE_KEY_ALIAS
      keyPassword MYAPP_RELEASE_KEY_PASSWORD
    }
  }
  buildTypes {
    release {
      ...
      signingConfig signingConfigs.release
    }
  }
}
...
```

Note that here we're using the variables we defined earlier in ~/.gradle/gradle.properties.

OK! Now we're ready to generate our signed APK.

Start the React Native Packager in your terminal, from the project root:

```
$ npm start
```

Again, from the project root, run the following commands:

```
$ mkdir -p android/app/src/main/assets
$ curl \
"localhost:8081/index.android.bundle?platform=android&dev=false&minify=true" \
    -o "android/app/src/main/assets/index.android.bundle"
$ cd android  && ./gradlew assembleRelease
```

Whoa, what's going on here? First, we're creating an *assets/* directory to store our bundled JavaScript. Then we're fetching the bundled JavaScript from the React Native Packager via a `curl` command. Finally, we're using `gradlew` to build our release APK.

This Procedure Might Change!

The React Native team has indicated that this procedure might change in future versions of React Native, as curling a special URL isn't the most intuitive process. As always, consult the official docs (*http://bit.ly/1NLqElP*).

After this, you can kill the React Native Packager; your bundled JavaScript has been saved to disk.

From the *android/* directory of your project, run the following command to install your signed APK:

```
./gradlew installRelease
```

This will install the signed APK onto your device.

As always before deploying, you'll want to test your application. For starters, you can upload this APK to an emulator or a plugged-in physical device using the `gradlew installRelease` command.

Distributing via Email or Other Links

Did you know that you don't actually need to deploy your application the Play Store in order to distribute it to Android users? In a pinch—or for testing—you can just distribute the APK file to users via email. Opening the email from an Android device will give users the ability to install it.

Your APK file is located at *android/app/build/outputs/apk/app-release.apk*. You can confirm that your release APK was successfully built by checking that the file exists:

```
$ ls android/app/build/outputs/apk/
app-debug-unaligned.apk  app-debug.apk
app-release-unaligned.apk  app-release.apk
```

Emailing that file to your users will allow them to download and install it. In fact, linking to this APK from anywhere, and opening that link from Android, will allow users to install your application.

One caveat: you'll first need to enable application installs from unknown sources. Check the Android docs on unknown sources (*http://bit.ly/1N4fxUC*) for more information.

Submitting Your Application to the Play Store

After you've had some time to test your release APK on a real device (or, hopefully, multiple devices), you're ready to deploy to the Google Play Store. All right!

This process is relatively painless, and review is pretty quick, too; you can expect to have your application deployed within 24 hours after submitting.

Begin by navigating to *http://developer.android.com* and clicking on Developer Console in the top-right corner of the page (Figure 11-3).

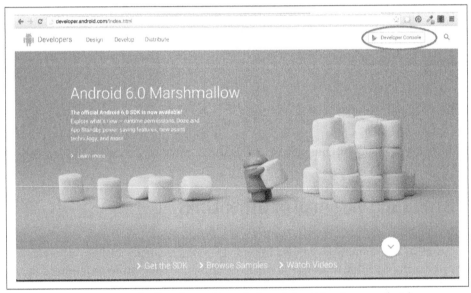

Figure 11-3. Navigate to the Developer Console from http://developer.android.com

If you don't already have a developer account, you'll need to make one, and accept Google's terms and conditions. Then, click the Android icon on the lefthand menu to view the Applications menu.

Click the "+ Add new application" button to create your application (Figure 11-4).

Figure 11-4. Adding a new application

Here, you'll be given the option of either uploading an APK first, or editing your Play Store listing. Either is fine.

To upload your APK, find the release APK on your file system—it should be in *android/app/build/outputs/apk/app-release.apk* (Figure 11-5).

Figure 11-5. Select your app-release.apk file

Once your APK file is uploaded, you can fill out the rest of your Play Store listing, or set up Beta Testing.

Beta Testing via the Play Store

The Google Play Store provides easy beta testing functionality. Once you've uploaded your APK, select the Beta Testing tab to start adding beta testers (Figure 11-6).

Figure 11-6. Beta Testing options in the Play Store

You have a few options here:

Open Beta Testing
With this option, users can join the program via a special link

Closed Beta Testing
This allows you to add individual users via their email address

Beta Testing Using Google Groups or Google+ Communities
This option allows members of your special Google Group to join the beta test

Google then makes it easy to distribute your APK to these users.

Even more so than with iOS, for Android you'll want to get your app into the hands of as many users as possible, because there's so much variation in devices. For example, Zebreto, a React Native application built with the default settings, is listed as compatible with *7,867* different devices according to the Play Store (Figure 11-7). Yikes!

Figure 11-7. The Play Store will helpfully indicate which devices your application supports

Different devices mean different screen sizes and resolutions, different features, and even differences in styling—some manufacturers apply their own skins on top of Android's default UI. Take advantage of the Beta Testing option!

Play Store Listing

Your Play Store listing includes important information about your application (e.g., its title, description, category, content rating, etc.). You'll need to fill out most of these fields in order to release your application.

The developer console will helpfully provide you with a list of remaining tasks if you click on the "Why can't I publish?" link (Figure 11-8).

Figure 11-8. Pending tasks that must be completed before publishing

As you work through the various required tasks, the checkmarks in the menu on the lefthand side will turn green. Finally, once you've completed all the necessary steps, the "Publish app" button will be enabled.

Required Assets for the Store Listing

As part of your Play Store listing, you'll need to upload some image assets (Figure 11-9). These include:

- At least two screenshots from your application
- A 512x512 pixel PNG version of your application's icon
- A 1024x500 pixel JPG or PNG "feature image" for the Play Store

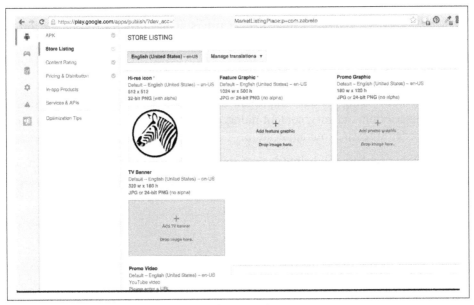

Figure 11-9. Uploading graphics to the Play Store listing

There are also some other, optional images, too, such as the Promo Graphic and Promo Video.

Remember that these assets are critical to your application's success on the Play Store!

If you don't already have screenshots, it's time to take some. You have two options here: taking screenshots from a physical device, or using an emulator. You can take screenshots on a physical device by holding down the power and volume-down buttons at the same time.

Taking screenshots from the emulator is a bit more complicated. First, make sure that your emulator has storage allocated for an SD card file. (You can do this by running `android avd` and then selecting "Edit" to view the emulator's specifications.)

Then, you can take screenshots using the adb shell:

```
adb shell screencap -p /sdcard/screen.png
adb pull /sdcard/screen.png
adb shell rm /sdcard/screen.png
```

These commands will take a screenshot, then pull them onto your local filesystem.

If you'd prefer a one-liner, try the following command:[1]

```
adb shell screencap -p | perl -pe 's/\x0D\x0A/\x0A/g' > screen.png
```

This will copy your screenshot into *screen.png* on your local filesystem.

Publishing Your Application

Ready to submit your application? As shown in Figure 11-10, go ahead and hit the "Publish app" button!

Figure 11-10. Publishing your application to the Play Store

After submitting your application for review, your application status will switch to pending, as you can see in Figure 11-11.

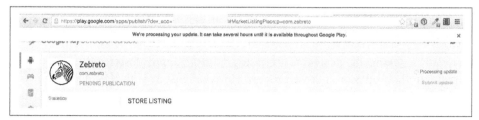

Figure 11-11. Application pending review

You should typically hear back within 24 hours. Afterward, your application will be available to the public via the Play Store—congratulations! See Figure 11-12. Go ahead and bask in the glory of your publicly available, complete Android application.

---

1 The one-line version comes to us courtesy of shvestov's blog (*http://bit.ly/1MxOK61*). Head there if you're curious about why we need to use Perl.

Figure 11-12. The Zebreto application, live on the Play Store

Summary

By this point, you should be equipped to release your React Native applications through both the Google Play Store and the iOS App Store!

Generally speaking, the process for releasing Android apps is faster and simpler, compared with the App Store release process. However, just as with iOS, deploying your application is just the beginning. You should plan on how you'll support your Android application postrelease, and just as with iOS, you should not assume that users will have auto-updating turned on for your application. Additionally, Android users have a huge range of devices with diverse specifications, so user testing each version is even more important on Android.

Conclusion

If you've made it this far, congratulations!

We've gone from creating your very first React Native application all the way up through deploying a cross-platform application to both the iOS App Store and the Google Play Store. In order to do so, we started by looking at the basic components for React Native, and how to style them. We learned how to work with touch and platform native APIs, like the Camera Roll and Geolocation APIs. We covered how to debug React Native applications with the developer tools, and how to deploy your applications to real devices. For functionality beyond the standard React Native library, we also saw how to use native Objective-C and Java modules as well as third-party JavaScript libraries using npm.

Your knowledge of JavaScript and React, coupled with the topics we've covered in this book, should enable you to quickly and efficiently write cross-platform mobile applications for Android and iOS. Of course, there's still plenty to learn, and this single book can't cover *all* the things you'll need to know in order to develop mobile applications with React Native. If you get stuck or have questions, reach out to the community, whether that's on Stack Overflow (*http://stackoverflow.com/questions/tagged/ react-native*) or on IRC (*irc://chat.freenode.net/reactnative*).

Keep in touch! Join the Learning React Native mailing list at LearningReactNative.com (*http://learningreactnative.com*) for more resources and updates related to the book. You can also find me on Twitter as @brindelle (*http://twitter.com/brindelle*).

Finally, and most importantly, have fun! I'm looking forward to seeing what you build.

ES6 Syntax

Some of the code samples in this book use what's known as ES6 syntax. If you're not familiar with ES6 syntax, don't worry—it's a pretty straightforward translation from the JavaScript you might be accustomed to.

ES6 refers to ECMAScript 6, also known as "Harmony," the forthcoming version of ECMAScript. JavaScript is an implementation of ECMAScript. There's plenty of interesting history behind these naming conventions, but what you need to know is: ES6 is the "new" version of JavaScript, and extends the existing specification with some helpful new features.

React Native uses Babel (*https://babeljs.io/*), the JavaScript compiler, to transform our JavaScript and JSX code. One of Babel's features is its ability to compile ES6 syntax into ES5-compliant JavaScript, so we can use ES6 syntax throughout our React codebase.

Destructuring

Destructuring assignments (*http://mzl.la/1I6ppBl*) provide us with a convenient shorthand for extracting data from objects.

Take this ES5-compliant snippet:

```
var myObj = {a: 1, b: 2};
var a = myObj.a;
var b = myObj.b;
```

We can use destructuring to do this more succinctly:

```
var {a, b} = {a: 1, b: 2};
```

You'll often see this used with `require` statements. When we `require` React, we're actually getting out an object. We *could* name components using the syntax, as shown in Example A-1.

Example A-1. Importing the <View> component without destructuring

```
var React = require('react-native');
var View = React.View
```

But it's much nicer to use destructuring, as shown in Example A-2.

Example A-2. Using destructuring to import the <View> component

```
var { View } = require('react-native');
```

Importing Modules

Normally, we might use CommonJS module syntax to export our components and other JavaScript modules (Example A-3). In this system, we use `require` to import other modules, and assign a value to `module.exports` in order to make a file's contents available to other modules.

Example A-3. Requiring and exporting modules using CommonJS syntax

```
var OtherComponent = require('./other_component');

var MyComponent = React.createClass({
  ...
});

module.exports = MyComponent;
```

With ES6 module syntax (*http://mzl.la/21cv5QF*), we can use the `export` and `import` commands instead. Example A-4 shows the equivalent code, using ES6 module syntax.

Example A-4. Importing and exporting modules using ES6 module syntax

```
import OtherComponent from './other_component';

var MyComponent = React.createClass({
  ...
});

export default MyComponent;
```

Function Shorthand

ES6's function shorthand (*http://mzl.la/1SW4AJ4*) is also convenient. In ES5-compliant JavaScript, we define functions as shown in Example A-5.

Example A-5. Longhand function declaration

```
render: function() {
  return <Text>Hi</Text>;
}
```

Writing out `function` over and over again can get annoying. Example A-6 shows the same function, this time applying ES6's function shorthand.

Example A-6. Shorthand function declaration

```
render() {
  return <Text>Hi</Text>;
}
```

Fat Arrow Functions

In ES5-compliant JavaScript, we often need to `bind` our functions to make sure that their context (i.e., the value of `this`) is as expected (Example A-7). This is especially common when dealing with callbacks.

Example A-7. Binding functions manually with ES5-compliant JavaScript

```
var callbackFunc = function(val) {
  console.log('Do something');
}.bind(this);
```

Fat arrow functions (*http://mzl.la/1MN2cRj*) are automatically bound, so we don't need to do that ourselves (Example A-8).

Example A-8. Using a fat-arrow function for binding

```
var callbackFunc = (val) => {
  console.log('Do something');
};
```

String Interpolation

In ES5-compliant JavaScript, we might build a string by using code such as that in Example A-9.

Example A-9. String concatenation in ES5-compliant JavaScript

```
var API_KEY = 'abcdefg';
var url = 'http://someapi.com/request&key=' + API_KEY;
```

ES6 provides us with tempate strings (*http://mzl.la/21cvceS*), which support multiline strings and string interpolation. By enclosing a string in backticks, we can insert other variable values using the ${} syntax (Example A-10).

Example A-10. String interpolation in ES6

```
var API_KEY = 'abcdefg';
var url = `http://someapi.com/request&key=${API_KEY}`;
```

Commands and Quickstart Guide

This appendix serves as a reference for some handy commands when working with React Native projects.

Creating a New Project

```
react-native init MyProject
```

Running on iOS

Open *ios/MyProject.xcodeproj* in Xcode. Click the Play button in the top-left. The React Native Packager should launch, as well as the iOS simulator.

Taking Screenshots on iOS

From the iOS simulator, pressing Command+S will save a screenshot to your desktop.

On a physical device, press the power and home buttons at the same time.

Running on Android

First, make sure you have an eligible device available.

To start an emulator, run:

```
android avd
```

Either create a new Android Virtual Device, or select an existing one and hit the Start... button.

Alternatively, you can attach a device via USB with USB debugging enabled. To enable USB debugging, go to Settings → About Phone → Build Number. Tap the Build Number seven times, until the device asks if you would like to enable development mode, and select "yes."

Once you have completed either of those steps, run:

```
react-native run-android
```

This will install your application on the device and start the React Native Packager.

Taking Screenshots on Android

You can take screenshots on a physical device by holding down the power and volume-down buttons at the same time.

To take screenshots from the emulator: ensure that your emulator has SD card storage enabled. Then use the adb shell:

```
adb shell screencap -p /sdcard/screen.png
adb pull /sdcard/screen.png
adb shell rm /sdcard/screen.png
```

Alternatively, use the following abbreviated command:

```
adb shell screencap -p | perl -pe 's/\x0D\x0A/\x0A/g' > screen.png
```

Running the React Native Packager

If, for some reason, you need to start the React Native Packager manually, navigate to your project's root directory and run:

```
npm start
```

Index

About the Author

Bonnie Eisenman is a software engineer at Twitter with previous experience at Code-cademy, Google, and Fog Creek Software. She has spoken at several conferences on topics ranging from React to musical programming and Arduinos. In her spare time, she enjoys building electronic musical instruments, laser-cutting chocolate, and learning languages.

Colophon

The animal on the cover of *Learning React Native* is a ringtail possum (*Pseudocheirus peregrinus*), a marsupial that is native to Australia. Ringtail possums are herbivorous and live primarily in forested regions. It is named for its prehensile tail, which is often coiled at the tip.

Ringtail possums are grey-brown in color, and can grow up to 35 centimeters in length. The diet of the ringtail possum consists of a variety of leaves, flowers, and fruits. They are nocturnal, and live in communal nests known as dreys. As marsupials, ringtail possums carry their young in pouches until they are developed enough to survive on their own.

The ringtail possum population declined steeply in the 1950s, but has recovered in recent years. However, they are still at risk of habitat loss due to deforestation.

Many of the animals on O'Reilly covers are endangered; all of them are important to the world. To learn more about how you can help, go to *animals.oreilly.com*.

The cover image is from *Shaw's Zoology*. The cover fonts are URW Typewriter and Guardian Sans. The text font is Adobe Minion Pro; the heading font is Adobe Myriad Condensed; and the code font is Dalton Maag's Ubuntu Mono.

Have it your way.

Get even more for your money.

Join the O'Reilly Community, and register the O'Reilly books you own. It's free, and you'll get:

- $4.99 ebook upgrade offer
- 40% upgrade offer on O'Reilly print books
- Membership discounts on books and events
- Free lifetime updates to ebooks and videos
- Multiple ebook formats, DRM FREE
- Participation in the O'Reilly community
- Newsletters
- Account management
- 100% Satisfaction Guarantee

Signing up is easy:

1. Go to: oreilly.com/go/register
2. Create an O'Reilly login.
3. Provide your address.
4. Register your books.

Note: English-language books only

To order books online:
oreilly.com/store

For questions about products or an order:
orders@oreilly.com

To sign up to get topic-specific email announcements and/or news about upcoming books, conferences, special offers, and new technologies:
elists@oreilly.com

For technical questions about book content:
booktech@oreilly.com

To submit new book proposals to our editors:
proposals@oreilly.com

O'Reilly books are available in multiple DRM-free ebook formats. For more information:
oreilly.com/ebooks